Fishing In Wild Places

David Street

Foreword by Ted Hughes
Poet Laureate

Illustrated by Terence Lambert

First published in 1989 by
The Golden Grove Book Company Limited
This edition first published by
the Gomer Press

Published in 1990 by
H. F. & G. WITHERBY LTD
14 Henrietta Street, London WC2E 8QJ

ISBN 0 85493 206 2

Printed in Wales
by Gomer Press, Llandysul
and bound
by WBC Maesteg

In memory of my late father
who first planted my young steps
'far in a western brookland'

Many of the stories that comprise the chapters of this book have appeared in different form as articles in the following journals:

Countrysport, Fisherman, Northwest Orient Airlines in-flight Magazine, The Irish Times, The Scotsman, Shooting Times & Country Magazine, Trout and Salmon, Trout Fisherman.

We acknowledge with thanks the permission of the editors of these publications to reproduce some of their copyright material.

Foreword

Ted Hughes
Poet Laureate

Fishing in Wild Places is a strangely absorbing book. David Street's lifelong infatuation with trout fishing has been acute enough, but he has an altogether unusual knack for conveying the haunted glamour of it.

Illustrations

Contents

Away to the Hills

A good many years ago I visited the lonely isle of Foula, Britain's remotest inhabited island with a population of 45. A raw Atlantic swell was buffeting the starboard bow of the little postboat, out from Scalloway, making her yaw and pitch at the ocean's whim, like a cork tossed at random on a river's current. If the motion caused was somewhat uncomfortable, the prospect before us was full of promise, bound as we were for the wind-swept isle, bringing mail and provisions for the doughty inhabitants, who would soon be scanning the horizon for a first-sighting of this vital life-link. Fishing boats were returning to harbour, trailing their clouds of gulls, raucous in anticipation of a bounty to be shared.

On the island, I noticed a small loch at the foot of the mountain with good trout rising all over it, and of course I had not brought my rod. All I could do was to gaze at it with longing. I was soon joined by another young fellow, and could tell from the expression on his face that he was in the same situation as I. He too was a fisherman without a rod, and one of a party of ornithologists on the island to count 'the bonxies'—great skuas—which have their largest breeding colony there.

Today, I know that the only person who ever fishes that place is Ross Gear, the young son of an island crofter, who has recently left school and is now trying to make a living for himself on the island. The fish, loch levens, were introduced as fingerlings many years ago by his great uncle. Some of them are now 3-4lbs in weight. Ross's favourite time to be beside the loch is 3.00 am on a calm summer's morning.

The nearest one will come to that sort of virgin trout-water on mainland Britain is likely to be in the remote uplands—tiny streams and mountain lochs in the wide country, where golden eagles sweep the skies and ospreys dive. Such places are fished, if at all, by only a handful of anglers in the course of a season, men prepared to travel light, to walk and climb for half the day and to make their way safely home in the evening without troubling the mountain rescue teams! As I have found out to my cost, the mist can come down quickly in these places, cocooning one in a cold, wet blanket of nothingness, the landscape disappears and it is hard even to trace one's own boots.

My love for this kind of adventurous fishing goes back to my youth and school holidays, when I would leave my beloved river to explore the even smaller streams that fed their waters into it. These were the real rivers of Lilliput, often so little that one could jump across them; streams whose brief and deep-cut courses had been fashioned in the Ice Age. Nurtured by mountain springs and draining the hills, they never ran dry, and often their fall was considerable.

One of the most exciting of these was the Maes y Gamfa stream which joined the little river Angell a mile above Cefngwyn, the holiday house my father bought in central Wales in 1936. This fell away from the mountain, through a spectacular rocky gorge in a whole series of cascades, each one of which had chiselled out a deep pool beneath it. Fishing up this ravine was an exercise in rock climbing, aided by the roots and branches of mountain ash, small whippy trees, which seemed to spring out of the barren rock face and gave one leverage. Both hands were called for and, even without a rod, it was difficult enough. The best times were always after heavy rain with the water still showing colour, and the fish matched the challenge—lovely, speckled mountain trout with short, deep bodies. It was one such expedition to fish these waters of Lilliput that was my first, real introduction to Fraser.

He was a canny Scot, whose accent sounded strange in our valley. He lived in the forester's lodge not far from where the Angell joined the River Dovey, and was himself a notable sewin (Welsh: sea-trout) fisherman, both with the worm in heavy water and also with the fly on the wider pools of the Dovey when the sun had set. At Machynlleth—the main town in the Dovey valley—a yellow flag is flown at the town hall to show that the worm may be fished in the river. Surely, a civilized type of town!

Being the head forester for the Forestry Commission, Fraser oversaw all the workings in the forests and would cover many miles on foot each day. On the day in question he had invited me and my brother, John, to go with him as he set out on his rounds. He was to leave us at the top of the Cwm Gerwyn mountain to fish the little streams that had their sources there and ran down the far side. No-one surely ever fished these out of the way places, and it was all new country to us.

Leaving our house in the early morning, our rods in their bags, two tins of worms and food for the day, we crossed the Angell by an ancient, wooden bridge, always shadowed dark by trees. Story had it that this place was haunted by a pack of phantom hounds. In the depth of the night people had heard their ghostly baying— such howling as froze the blood. Even on summer days, when the sun shone bright, the place possessed a cold and sinister aspect. I had also noticed that no birds nested here—it was a perfect place for a dipper or a wagtail to rear its brood—but, whenever I had fished the pool beneath, I had caught nothing but eels. I too had come to believe that it probably was haunted.

From there we followed the track up Cwm Caws (the valley of the cheese), passing several small forestry holdings and then Cwmllecoediog Hall, the one big house in our valley. The track now became very steep, as it climbed further and further into the dark heart of the forest. Finally, we crossed the watershed, and soon the jingle of new-sprung waters told us it was time to part company and go our separate ways. Fraser wished us 'tight lines' and carried on in search of his gangs. John and I hurriedly put up our rods and it was not long before our worms were searching out each little glide and overhang in the tiny streams. So absorbed did we become in our sport that we soon parted company and never met up again, each of us choosing to follow different water courses.

Time never passes faster than when you are fishing, and we quite forgot that the further we followed the waters down, the further we were getting from home. The day was fine, buzzards mewed overhead as they spiralled lazily in the warm air, and little dippers bowed to us from their rocky perches in the ever-widening streams. The pools grew bigger as we went and their voices more enticing. They were, in fact, acting like the dreaded sirens, whose ancient music had lured the hapless sailors to their fate. The sun sets very quickly in the mountains. One minute it is there, the next it has gone, and it must have been this sudden change of light that made me stop and look up. The western sky was afire with a red afterglow, and a pale crescent moon had replaced the sun. The day was well and truly spent. Loath, as always, to put down the rod, it was already way past time to be setting out for home. I had finished up close by the village of Aberllefenni, a whole mountain away from Cefngwyn. There was still enough light, as I thought, to trace the river up again, then over the top to drop down on the far side. But my easy reckoning had taken no account of the fast-encroaching night, nor of the true contours of Cwm Gerwyn. The forest added yet further to the blackness and soon one small boy was lost in the vastness of the hills.

Neither my brother nor I had taken map or compass when we started the day, but with the bright morning, the excitement of the sport ahead and Fraser to go with us, who thinks of getting lost? In any case, it was too dark now for map or compass to have helped. As the crow flies I was not more than four miles from home, but it was not the night for me to impersonate the crow. I tramped around for miles, sometimes in circles only to return to where I had been before. At no stage was I frightened. In fact, I would have traded even my bag of trout to have been standing there and then on that black and haunted bridge. One thing only troubled me, the anxiety I would be causing at home.

In a strange way the experience seemed to stimulate me, summoning as it did, unexplored resources from deep within me. It was then that I remembered the compass in the sky, the Pole-star, and soon I hit the track we had travelled in the morning. I suppose I should have been laughing all the way now, but for one thing: that fateful bridge still lay before me. I had never been at it, or anywhere near it, in the midnight hour before. Were those hounds of the Baskervilles waiting there for me?

6

By now my resolve was made. No point in trying to creep furtively across—nor even to divert and wade the river further downstream; the knees were weak, the sweat ran down my arms, the heart pounded. There was only one thing for it—and that was to take it by storm. To shatter the stillness of the night: to scare the living nightlights out of any lurking hounds. One of my favourite books from nursery days had possessed the stirring title of *Fights for the Flag*, a book which, in heroic narrative and vivid illustration, told the story of some of the most glorious episodes in British arms. Now I recalled Rourke's Drift and, summoning the blood, charged the bridge at full speed, uttering a brave fiendish warcry as I went.

I was still panting when I finally reached home. It was now well past midnight and my brother had been equally lost, which was some consolation. He had arrived shortly before me. Fraser's day had long been over, but he too was at the house and, with father, was about to set out again in search. Soon, his forester's boots removed, he settled down with his pipe and a large whisky and, with us boys tucking into bacon and eggs, the conversation turned to sewin.

Despite those phantom hounds, the fatal fascination for distant, seldom-fished waters has always remained, and was soon to be boosted by a new discovery I was about to make. Not far from our house was a small pond, known as the Bathing Pool, which belonged to Sir Ernest Bennett, a distinguished, former member of parliament and the owner of the big house, Cwmllecoediog Hall. He had had a dam built across one of the small tributaries of the river Angell in order to make a place where his children could swim with their friends. But, by the time we came to know it, it had long since given up this function.

It now stood unvisited and unloved and surrounded by a three-stranded, barbed wire fence, its bottom covered by black pungent mud. At the opposite end to the dam, weed had colonized this mud where an old diving board pointed drunkenly towards the sky. The shrieks and laughter of bathing children had given way to gentler sounds. Above the meadow, dogs barked from the forestry holdings, wagtails uttered shrill cries as they ran along the top of the dam wall, disturbing dragonflies, which lazed in the sun, with, here and there, the plop of a feeding trout. These were the little trout of the burn, now grown fat and prosperous in the luxury of their deep and wide, weed-fringed pool.

My father, in his usual way, had very soon made friends with Sir Ernest and Lady Bennett. With many years of teaching at Shrewsbury behind him, and gifted with an exceptional memory, he always seemed to me to possess one great advantage when meeting new people for the first time. It was not just the names of generations of boys that he remembered so well, but also details of their families too and, as often as not, particular incidents and occasions, often trivial ones, connected with them. I am pretty sure that he would not have been talking to Sir Ernest for very long, before they discovered several friends in common. It always seemed to work out like this, and his happy knack frequently produced spin-offs, which were much to our advantage. My brother, John, and I were given permission to fish the Bathing Pool more or less when we wanted.

It certainly turned out to be an interesting place to fish, not least because of the difficulties it presented—the main one being to find

a suitable stance from which to cast. The end by the dam was virtually unfishable because of the tall trees behind, though a sidecast here with a short line was just possible. I had yet to learn the merits of the roll cast. Mud and weeds had made the far end by the diving board completely inaccessible.

This left the two sides, where there still remained the skeletal timber frames of what once had been three bathing platforms. Two of these contained some sort of base and could be mounted gingerly at one's peril, though even this caused them to sway uncertainly. Even so, they provided the best positions, and seemed almost to challenge you to try and fish from them. An over-eager cast from either and you could easily end up with your fly entwined in the telephone lines above, your lower parts impaled on barbed wire and your face firmly imprinted in the ooze below.

The secret of success lay in spotting a rising trout and endeavouring to present a floating fly to him as delicately as possible. I always hoped for a gentle breeze, just enough to ripple the surface of the water. For this breath of air imparted its own life to the fly, making it dance invitingly on top, and, by cutting down reflections, helped to conceal the gut, which otherwise appeared to lie, like a hawser, on the surface. If the fish did not take it at once, the fly could be left for a short time as the ripple moved it slowly across the water. A rising trout on stillwater is usually a cruising trout.

The excitement of covering a fish that had just risen was so intense that the body began to tremble, as the nerves and muscles became suddenly charged by a higher voltage that speeded every action. An older head than mine would now have steadied himself before casting, but, in the early years, this sudden new impulse, which the trout had generated, frequently played havoc with my cast, causing my fly to land with a splash or in clumsy coils of gut. No self-respecting trout would rise to this, nor indeed to anything else, until his fright had subsided. If, however, I did contrive to land my fly nicely, the chances were that he would have it, and this put the rickety old bathing platform to a still greater test.

No wonder that, whenever we approached this pool across the sloping fields, our eyes would scan it keenly, and any signs of a rise would quicken our steps into a scarcely concealed run. The Bathing Pool, however, delighted in playing tricks, and often marsh gas, bubbling up from the muddy bottom, would bring us breathless to its verges.

I soon found that the trout from this pool were larger than those we caught in the streams. They were certainly nothing spectacular and I do not think we ever caught one that was more than half a pound, but that was twice the weight of the biggest trout we could hope for in the Angell. I noticed too that fish from the pool were different in colour from those of the river. Even the river fish varied from place to place; ones from deep, rockbound pools tended to be dark fish, whereas those from shallower, sandy lies would be much brighter and more golden. The Bathing Pool trout still showed the same basic markings, but his overall hue was more of an olive green. The size a trout attains will depend upon the feeding available to him; his coloration on the nature of the ground and the general environment in which he lives.

My discovery that pond or lake trout were, on the whole, larger than trout from the rivers may not have been as dramatic as some that history has recorded, but to my young, fishing mind it was a real breakthrough. Had not God himself posed the question to Job, 'Cans't thou draw out Leviathan with an hook?' The answer then was that he certainly could not. But what limits had been set to the size a wild trout might attain, and, in the fastnesses of the hills, who knew what mighty fish swam in the deep places of the lakes to be found there? I had recently caught my first sewin in the little river, and this too had whetted my appetite for bigger game. Both these factors now combined to determine the next birthday present I would buy for my father, a choice that I must confess was not devoid of a measure of self-interest. For the price of a shilling, I picked up in a second-hand bookshop a book entitled *The Lakes of Wales* by Frank Ward.

Printed in 1931, it proved a veritable mine of information, and up to the start of the War was destined to inspire many happy, family expeditions. The author had certainly done his research well, recording over five hundred lakes, some two hundred of which he had fished personally in the course of many, roving holidays. Map location, access, height above sea level, type of fish contained, whether fishing was private or free, from whom permission could be sought, average size of fish, scenery, all were recorded.

From the earliest time many had been places of veneration, where on the 'Spirit Nights' the Druids had celebrated their Arkite mysteries. Some possessed lovely, visionary names—such as 'The Well of the Moon' or 'The Lake of the Floating Islands'—which conjured up the magic of their wild locations; others, names which recalled ancient legends and practices associated with them, and, where possible, Ward had recounted these as well.

This new-found bible not only introduced me to fishing the remote lochs of the hills, but also planted in my young imagination the possibilities of strange wonders that could transcend normal life. On several occasions in later life, whilst fishing in such places, I have found myself suddenly arrested by a strong awareness of the numinous, a profoundly mystical experience, as though unseen influences were at play upon me, transporting my spirit into new, bright realms of ecstasy and well-being.

A wind steals from the mountain, pirouettes on spirit toes across the surface of the lake, breathes life into the waters; they darken at the touch, begin to move and then to murmur, their voices turn to lullaby as they lap the shore in soft embrace. The wind is spirit and the water is life. From distant straths the fluting wail of curlews trembles on the air, a raven barks and echoing crags give back the cry, peewits wheel and, tumbling through the skies, spill their lamentations on the wind. The raucous traffic of the world is silenced and, in the stillness, we listen to primordial sounds, which fall upon our ears from beyond the far horizons of history. They invoke immense perspectives in time, as they stir our spirits, and bind us in a unifying ring of life to ancient peoples, who trekked and hunted here before the Druids.

We must at all costs preserve these places as they are the last, few, remaining wilderness areas that are left in our land. Unprofitable in terms of finance they may be, but what profit to the soul. This is a sacred pledge we owe to all the generations yet to come.

One of our first expeditions was to Llyn Coch Hwyad, 1,500 feet up and some six miles south east of Dinas Mawddwy. Translated, its name means 'The Red Lake of the Ducks', and Ward describes it as containing many pike and a few large trout. We were decidedly naughty on this occasion, as he went on to point out that permits to fish were at one time obtainable but fishing was now private, being let with the shooting.

The lake, however, was sufficiently remote, the lure of large trout enticing and the worst we could suffer would be a peppering with shot. We managed to avoid the latter fate, but still paid the penalty for our boldness—no trout took the slightest interest in our flies. There was never a duck in sight and the lake was decidedly grey.

The long holidays of 1939 proved to be the last of the summer and what a vintage summer it turned out to be. Although black and menacing storm-clouds were building daily and already beginning to lour over Europe, they cast few, if any, shadows across my path as yet. Anyway, with my fifteenth birthday now behind me, my apprenticeship to the gentle craft was still far from completed.

Unexpected visitors were nothing unusual when we were at Cefngwyn, and so it was no real surprise when my headmaster, Henry Kendall, suddenly turned up out of the blue. Not knowing of his impending arrival, we had already laid plans for an outing on the following day to Llyn Nant Ddeiliog, which lay on the high ground in some very wild country between Llanbrynmair and Llanidloes. Alec Binney, a colleague of my father's at Shrewsbury, and no mean fisherman himself, was already staying with us, and as the whole family wanted to go, we were going to be a large party, with four rods fishing. The date was September 2nd, and by now the German storm-troops were already massed on the Polish frontiers, a factor which decided my headmaster to return to Oxford. Before he left, however, he made a wager that we would not catch a dozen trout—the stake was half a crown and, to win it, we had to send a dozen fish tails to him by the next available post.

The book informed us that this lake held numerous trout up to three quarters of a pound, but fishing there was erratic and a steady south wind was favoured. Lying 1,650 feet up it was likely to fish better late on in the season, as the waters at this altitude were slow to warm.

Leaving the Dovey valley at Cemmaes Road, we followed the River Twymyn almost to its source high on the Plynlimon range. It was a spectacular drive with the valley narrowing into a very deep gorge near the top. As we approached this gorge, the lush green meadows beside the river gradually gave way to the more sombre browns of the bare uplands, the home of sheep and ravens, mountain hares and hunting falcons. So sheer did the road fall away on one side that an uncle of mine, on another occasion, asked to be left out of the car; the poor man suffered from vertigo. The Twymyn is one of the more notable tributaries of the River Dovey, and enjoys a pretty fair run of sewin as well as its share of salmon. Near its confluence it passes through the little village of Commins Coch, once the home of notorious 'Red Brigands'. In earlier times this band had proved themselves a menace to travellers.

On one exploit they ambushed an English judge as he made his way home by coach from the assizes, after sentencing some Welshmen to hang—a life for a life, their crime had been to steal a sheep. It had taken place near the hairpin bend on the Mallwyd to Foel road by the bridge over the little Clywedog River. One could hardly have chosen a more perfect spot to lay an ambush, for besides the hairpin, which would bring a traveller to a virtual halt, the banks of the road are steep and wooded here. They brought the coach to a sudden stop by dropping a tree across its path, whereupon they killed the judge and made off into the fastnesses of the mountains.

The brigands derived their name from the fact that they were mostly red-headed. As a boy I rarely fished the Twymyn, as it was a good way from our home, but, on the one occasion that I did, I came across some of the local lads from Commins Coch, who were also after sewin, though by much less orthodox means. I noticed that the fiery hair still predominated, and wondered then if they were aware of their illustrious forebears. A well known fishing inn at Mallwyd is today called 'The Brigands Inn', which they must have passed on their way to the ambush.

Our route ended at the ghost town of Dylife where we left the cars. In its heyday this had been a thriving lead-mining centre, but now it lay abandoned and in ruins save for a few sturdy households and its memories. It did, however, possess a tiny pub called 'The Star', kept then by a charming old lady, who cannot possibly have had much trade, perhaps the odd shepherd, some walkers and a handful of regulars. It lay just off the road, which continued on to Machynlleth, and would hardly have caught the notice of summer tourists. To me, it seemed a magic little place, set alone among a cluster of Scots Firs, the only trees for miles. I suspect that its walls still ring with the choruses of miners long since departed.

The whole Plynlimon massif is one of the most extensive tracts of really wild country to be found in the Principality and the folk who lived up here were certainly cut off. The story is told of one old lady in Dylife who had not been much further than her gate for half a century. When told that war had broken out in 1939, she is reported to have asked, 'Haven't they caught that old Kruger yet?' One can believe it too.

Our trek to the lake passed 'The Star' and then two deserted chapels, not a hundred yards apart, where we startled the sheep inside and flushed an owl, before starting to ascend the plateau. The first sighting of a new lake is always exciting and seems to lend both urgency and energy to the climb, and Nant Ddeiliog was no disappointment when we found it. As we breasted the col there it was, lying before us like a bright blue gem set on a great cloth of green, shimmering in the sunlight. It was clearly a man-made lake, the south eastern end being formed by a gentle earth and shingle dam, which had none of the gauntness of the dark and forbidding reservoir wall. A tiny outlet trickled from this dam, gathering momentum as it went, before finally plunging in total abandonment down the rock gorge to lose itself in the waters of the Twymyn a mile away.

The day was warm, the air intoxicating and the scenery superb. Big, fleecy clouds kept bringing subtle changes to the light, which in turn played upon the colours of the landscape. A day of beauty, such as this, is over all too soon and we were quickly to our tasks, the fishermen to the water and the rest to scout for firewood. I have never really been keen on competitive trout fishing, but it is not every day that a boy can win half a crown from his headmaster. Wager or no wager, we were resolved to play it fair, and this meant that all undersized fish would be returned. As the day progressed, and with the rods scattered, there was no way of knowing how we were doing. I remember my sister Ann, who did not normally fish, claiming that she had caught one. At some stage she had picked up a rod and disappeared to the far corner of the dam. She failed to produce the fish, however, and there were no witnesses, but to this day she remains adamant, 'I had it on the beach, I had it on the beach'. Truth to tell, I think she nearly caught a small trout.

Then, as the shades began to lengthen and the early autumn evening to grow chill, three of us turned out our creels and laid out the catch. We counted eleven nice trout on the grass, though nothing more than half a pound. My brother John, however, was still not in. Clearly it was he who held the key to success or failure, but the signs were far from hopeful. He appeared to have abandoned fishing some hours ago and, when last seen, was stretched out on the grasses. Just at that moment the evening peace was shattered by a wild yell.

Certainly John was still alive, but what else it signified was anybody's guess. When he did finally appear, he was carrying the most awful-looking trout I have ever seen, long, thin and black, all head and tail and barely recognisable as one of the *salmo trutta* family. Clearly not fit to eat, it did, however, possess a handsome tail, and, at this stage, that was all that mattered. Weary of fly-fishing, John had settled down at the head of the lake, where a stream ran in, and here he had stripped the dressing from his fly-hook, grubbed up a worm and, leaving it to lie in the water, had apparently gone to sleep. We named this creature 'George', and it must have been a kindness to hit him on the head. George had saved the day.

At home that night, twelve fish tails were sealed in an envelope and in due course posted to Oxford. My headmaster paid his debt, but before those tails arrived Neville Chamberlain had told the nation, 'No such undertaking has been received. I therefore have to tell you that from 11 o'clock this morning we are at war with Germany'.

I vividly remember the sun that went down that day upon Nant Ddeiliog, how it had scattered its fire upon the mountain tops until the whole world seemed to be aflame. What I did not know then was that it had also set in blood.

Chapter 2

Gallantry on a Highland Loch

One Easter holidays, Mr Roodhouse, the parent of a boy in my father's house, invited both my father and me, together with his own son, Gerry, to fish with them in Scotland. Mr Roodhouse was a Lancastrian businessman of some repute and a most amusing character. The four of us travelled up by sleeper on the night train to Perth, our destination was to be Balquhidder, a small village in the Perthshire hills in the heart of the Rob Roy country. Here we were to stay with Jock and Mrs Stewart who, unable to sleep us all in their little cottage by the burn, gave me the luxury of a feather bed in a wee 'hoose' nearby.

Jock was an old man then, but still a wonderful ghillie who possessed a lifetime's experience of Loch Voil. At this early time of the year the loch water was still cold and we spent the days trolling a natural minnow. Gerry and I would get up well before breakfast in order to catch the day's supply of these in the little burn that splashed and tumbled behind the cottage, and they were later mounted onto small spinning flights. We made some nice baskets of trout, fishing this way, and what splendid fighters they were. Schooled, as I had been, on the mountain streams of Wales, it was a great thrill to play these fellows, which averaged a pound or more.

Jock himself had all the attributes of the very best of the old school of boatmen. Not given to much talk, he possessed the knack of radiating confidence and this, coupled with his great knowledge of the loch, made you expect fish, and, if you expect fish, you are always more likely to catch them, even if only trolling. If sport grew slow or non-existent Jock was likely to break the silence, 'Ach, I'll futch ye a fush by the black rock', and, sure enough, hardly before we had rounded the rock the reel would be singing once again. I cannot explain how this comes about; I only know that it happens, and that it is all a part of the mystery of fishing. Many a modern boatman, with his mind firmly on the 6.00 pm deadline, never suggests moving to new ground, and for no better reason than that it means more work; not so Jock who was seemingly tireless at the oars. Mrs Stewart, meanwhile, kept a good fire in the hearth and, as the evenings drew on with a distinct chill, this made a welcome homecoming. The trout were grilled in oatmeal, by which time they had become 'smokies', and delicious they were too.

Fishing all day from a boat can be somewhat cramping: the lunch break apart, there is little scope for stretching the legs, and the wooden seat grows harder on the backside. We were, therefore, quite pleased to give the loch a miss for one day and explore one of the many burns instead. We knew the fish would be less than half the size, much less, but the business of stalking and outwitting them would be heightened. Trolling, after all, calls for the minimum of skill and is usually a counsel of despair. As we greased our lines and put up the seven-foot rods on the stone bridge that spanned the burn, we felt a different kind of excitement. Beneath us, the little stream sang joyously as it wove its changing patterns in white froth upon a dark brown background. Drawing its lifeblood from the ancient peat, it looked for all the world like Guinness, and we chose our flies to match the water, putting up the Butcher and Black Zulu, and began to work our way upstream, using a very short line. The sport was fast and furious, as each little trout came with the speed of lightning, and many were missed.

Such rivers as these call for physical energy. Because the fishing is all close range, the successful angler must first know how to stalk, and this entails fieldcraft of a high order—bent body blending into background, and stealthy tread. Once the fish have taken fright, a cast, however brilliant, is of little use. Each twist and turn the river takes presents new problems to challenge the angler's craft, and he has always to read the water, note the wind and mark exactly where he wants to place his flies. Pinpoint accuracy is often needed. Sometimes, a sudden gust will lift the cast at the last moment, another will land it on the heather. Invariably a good trout lies in the shelter of the big boulder that divides the stream, but the swirling waters that form this brief refuge only allow the flies to work for a fraction of a second. To succeed here, wrist and eye must work together in perfect co-ordination. The faintest of checks on the line, or the golden gleam of a trout as he turns, are the only signs that will be given, and speed is everything. Then, at the end of the day, when the angler straightens his back and strides for home, his creel will be heavier by a dozen or so hard-earned fish. His limbs may ache, but his mind and spirit will have been renewed by the rhythms of the burn and beauty of the moorland. Memory will treasure the sounds and the scents of such a day.

The diversion on the river made us all the more eager for the loch again. Our holiday was coming to an end fast and the weather, which had been kind to us all through, continued to smile. Gerry and I had felt the early chill as we collected the minnows, but, by the time we reached the boat, the spring sun was warm upon our necks. Jock had everything prepared and was eager to set out. When he beached for lunch at the head of the loch, the day was already fulfilling its early promise, and five nice trout had come to the net.

Time has always been a puzzle to me, and never more so than in a day's fishing. Measured by clock and calendar it is constant and relentless, but measured in terms of our experience it is not like that at all. It can be both hare and tortoise, and a good day's fishing seems to bypass it almost completely. Perhaps we shall only understand its mystery when we ourselves have passed beyond its bounds.

This day was no exception. The hours had flown and already we were on the final drift, heading for the boathouse, our two rods still seeking for a last trout. It was then that Gerry's stuck fast and, with the boat under way, line began to strip from his reel. Although we had trolled the loch for many hours, this was the first occasion either of us had met an obstruction. Gerry appeared well and truly snagged and would soon be looking for new hooks. As Jock steadied the boat and I started to recover my line, Gerry's suddenly took off and began to cut the waters of the loch like a wire through cheese. Then the water erupted in front

of us and we had a full view of a magnificent salmon as it leapt clean and clear into the evening sky. Jock put the fish as being some eighteen to twenty pounds, and it made off like an express train. Gerry was quickly to his feet and holding on for all he was worth, but there was no holding the salmon. In no time the reel was onto the backing and still the fish ran. Jock, who had quickly turned the boat, began to row as we had never seen him row before, bending to the oars as if Old Nick was coming up astern. He chased and chased in a desperate attempt to keep in touch. Once the backing on the reel had been exhausted the fight would be over, and we all knew it.

The fish could have won the contest in that first wild rush, had he only known how close he was to victory. Instead, he chose to leap again and, throwing his silvered body in a splendid parabola, temporarily ceased his run. So the struggle continued, flight and chase, flight and chase.

I had checked my watch when the salmon first leapt—it was 5.35 pm, the sun was approaching the western horizon, but there was still plenty of light. Jock was well past man's allotted span of three score years and ten, and yet it would have been hard to choose which was the gamer, the old man or the salmon. He pursued him for a mile and more and still the runs continued.

An hour had now slipped by. The hooks were holding and the chances of boating our fish became a reality rather than an impossible dream. The question was how to do it? Our trout net was hopelessly inadequate and we had no other landing tackle. One possibility was to play the fish out in the deep water, then beach the boat and draw him gently onto the shore where he could be tailed by hand. Another rescue lay three hundred yards up the brae behind us. Here stood a croft, and Jock knew the folk that lived there.

Up to this point I had been a mere spectator and much enjoying my ringside seat, but now I was to earn my keep. I waded ashore and climbed up there to see if I could borrow a gaff. Unwilling to miss more of the contest than was necessary, I ran all of the way, finally arriving, breathless and perspiring, and told my story. My worst fears were soon confirmed. There was no gaff.

Behind the natural reserve of every Scot there lies a strong sporting instinct. The fact that he had no gaff should have been the end of it, except that I now noticed the reserve was starting to melt, as his somewhat bewildered expression, caused by the sudden appearance of a Sassenach and a mere boy at that, began to kindle into a brightening glow. Soon my new-found friend became interested and, finally, involved. He beckoned me to follow him across the rough yard and into the cow-byre at the far end, where, from the cobwebbed rafters above the stalls, he produced a large hook. This at least had the makings of a gaff, and, firmly bound with twine to a broom handle, it might yet save the day. My first disappointment turned to admiration and profound gratitude and, thanking him warmly, I raced down the brae, brandishing this strange device. Messrs Hardy Bros, of Alnwick, may have turned up their noses at it but, in the heat of battle, the weapons are what lie to hand.

The boat had moved out again, but I could see that the salmon was still in play. By the time I rejoined my comrades the fish was tiring fast, though by no means ready to be brought in close.

Gerry was puffing at yet another cigarette, in fact his fourth since the battle started. Normally he never smoked at all, at least not in public, so the strain was getting to him. Jock himself had already rowed his heart out. Being the only one unscarred, I decided to search the lunch-hamper to see if any whisky remained in the flask. This had been provided each day, mainly for Jock's benefit, for early on in the holiday we had found that, once he had moistened his lips with a dram of the White Horse, we would soon be finding trout again. Some did remain but, with the crisis stage approaching, it was not the best time to be passing it around. I decided to reserve it for the victory celebration or, more sombrely, resuscitation should our gallant boatman, who had given his all, suffer a cardiac arrest.

The sun had now dipped, and the last lingering streaks of day were following it fast. I glanced once more at my watch which was coming up to 7.30 pm: it had been an hour and fifty five minutes since our salmon first leapt clear, and still the 3X gut and trout-sized trebles were holding in the fish. Surely he must be ours now?

At last, Jock shipped the oars and rose wearily, and somewhat unsteadily, to his feet. Clutching now at the broom handle, more it seemed, as a prop for his aching back than anything else, he peered over into the darkness of the water, and there was the salmon wallowing lazily beside the boat. He looked massive. All that was needed now was to slip the hook quietly and gently into the water and lift him inboard. If any man knew this it must have been this old man, and yet it seemed that, in this final moment of the drama, all his experience deserted him. He let the gaff hit the water with such a splash that the startled fish gave one last violent kick, and three pairs of eyes followed him as he swam slowly, almost casually, into the darkness. Beneath a gibbous moon the wind's lament was lulled, the waters whispered and night's long arms reached out to enfold the blooded hero, who had fought so magnificently. Such blind valour was his heritage, and now he lived only to pass it on to another generation.

As I remember it, we saw the great fish go in silence. There were certainly no recriminations, no harsh words. Gerry shed a few quiet tears, but he was entitled to them. After all is said and done, fishing is first a sport, and the adversary must often win the day as well. A man who cannot lose a fish without bitterness is not a true fisherman. After that, it is a philosophy, one that binds its practitioners together in a strong brotherhood. The successes and disappointments, when they come, are there to be shared. We three had shared the comradeship of this endeavour, and now also what was left of the whisky. It is, as every Scotsman knows, the drink for all occasions; the dram that celebrates a victory is no less the dram that soothes a sorrow.

Since that battle on Loch Voil I have met and fished with many boatmen of all kinds. Today, I would have no hesitation in placing the late Jock Stewart of Balquhidder amongst the top three of them all, in spite of his gaffe with the gaff.

As we left Scotland at the end of the holiday I was coming up to my eighteenth birthday. In nine months time I had gained a regular commission in the Royal Marines, which meant that my apprenticeship to the craft of angling was therefore at an end. It was to be many years before my rods were to see action once again. There was, however, one final sortie, which came about in an unusual way.

My official rank was that of a Probationary Second Lieutenant, the lowest form of officer life known in the Corps. The whole of our first three years were spent in undergoing various courses in both naval and military subjects, undertaken at different bases and wide-ranging in content and character. Once these were safely over, one dropped the 'Probationary', and put up a second 'pip'. We were also taught, of course, how to conduct ourselves like officers and gentlemen. One of the niceties we had to observe was that of leaving our visiting cards with the Commander-in-Chief, whenever we arrived at a new station. My natural tendency, at this infant stage in my career, was to give all 'top brass' as wide a berth as possible. When calling, however, there was no need to disturb the C-in-C himself. There was always a silver salver provided in his entrance lobby, and etiquette was satisfied if one left one's card there. But I still prayed that I would not bump into the great man, coming out as I was going in. I had even thought up opening gambits for use if probationary second lieutenant and C-in-C ever came face to face—'Nice day for the war, sir'—but somehow none of them really commended themselves, and such naïvety laid one bare to a savage riposte.

On the occasion in question, I was at my home barracks at Eastney in Portsmouth, pursuing a course in naval gunnery at H.M.S. *Excellent* on Whale Island, the home of naval gunnery. The Admiral Superintendent of HM Dockyard, Portsmouth, at that time was Rear Admiral Clarke—later to become Admiral Sir Marshall Clarke—who was also a member of the governing body of St Edward's School, Oxford. He had sent his own son there and I had been his head of house only a few terms before. The Admiral had found out from somewhere, probably Michael, that I was at Eastney, and he very kindly invited me over to dinner one evening. He turned out to be a super fellow, who knew how to put a shy, young subaltern at ease, and I thoroughly enjoyed myself. During dinner the conversation got round to fishing, and the admiral mentioned that he had some water on the Hampshire Meon, not very far away. Once I got back to barracks I was to make considerable capital amongst my fellow subalterns over the fact that I had dined with the Admiral Superintendent of the Dockyard, so much so that one of them dared me to ring him up and ask permission to fish his beat on the River Meon.

The challenge was issued and I was left with little alternative but to accept. Anyhow, the admiral had been a friendly old soul and I did not feel I stood in much danger of a court-martial over it. I finally plucked up the courage to make the call after one of our guest night dinners. My resolve was undoubtedly fortified by the excellent wines and port—and by the splendid music of the Royal Marines' String Orchestra. I do not think I would have done it had I been stone-cold. I quit the ante-room and made my way to the mess telephone where I dialled the Superintendent's residence, to be answered by a chief petty officer. I asked if I could speak to the admiral.

'Who's calling, sir?'

'Will you tell him it is Second Lieutenant Street of the Royal Marines?'

'Aye, aye, sir.'

And off he went. I often wondered what that CPO thought. I imagined that most incoming calls would emanate from Churchill, or Eisenhower or, at least, the C-in-C. Presently I heard the phone picked up and a cheerful voice the other end.

'Hello David. What can I do for you?'

I was almost home and dry. I thanked him again for his hospitality of a few nights ago—I had already done so by letter— and then made my request. The port was now beginning to do its work, as only good port can, and I even went further and asked if I could take a Royal Marine colleague with me.

'Why of course', said the admiral.

'When do you want to go? There's no-one fishing it this Saturday. By all means take your brother officer along. I hope you have some sport. Let me know.'

When I returned to the mess ante-room the post-prandial revelries were getting under way, as well as somewhat out of hand. Only schoolboys on the last night of term can rival officers after a guest-night dinner at this kind of thing. I sought out my friend, David Langley, who had dared me to make the call in the first place. He too was a humble Second Lieutenant (Probationary) of the same term as myself, and destined later to win a Military Cross in the jungles of Malaya.

'Bet you haven't rung that admiral yet.'

'Oh yes, I have', I replied. 'In fact, I'm fishing his water on Saturday'.

I paused to let this sink in, and then added, as an after-thought. 'Oh by the way, he said I could bring the lad along as well'.

I was one up and with all to play for. In fact neither of us scored that Saturday, but then the Meon is a chalkstream, and I am sure we had not got the right flies, nor the local knowledge.

By the time I was to fish again the clouds had lifted over Europe and the Far East, and life for me had also taken several more of its unexpected turns.

Chapter 3

Twixt Fells and Sea

The counties of Tyne and Wear, Durham, Cleveland and North Yorkshire, which lie sandwiched between the north Pennines and the Cleveland Hills on the west and the North Sea on the east, form a comparatively unsung part of the country, and together present a region of striking contrasts. The high, desolate fells afford some of the wildest landscapes to be found anywhere in England, whilst the coastal strip, with the exception of North Yorkshire, remains heavily populated and contains the major industrial ports of Newcastle, Sunderland, Hartlepool and Middlesbrough.

The Pennine backbone is the birthplace of many waters, which drop from the hills in deep ghylls, gathering as they go to form fine rivers that wind through pleasant dales and farmlands before joining the sea. The three most important of these, the rivers Tyne, Wear and Tees, provided, at their mouths, the main arteries for the industrial prosperity which the region once generated—coal, iron and steel, heavy engineering, ship-building and armaments—a prosperity now sorely eroded by the economic changes, although North Sea oil and associated petrochemicals have compensated to some degree.

I first came across the Tees in the war years, when I arrived at Middlesbrough to take up the posting of Gunnery Control Officer on a gunboat that was being built there. After commissioning, we carried out our sea and gunnery trials, and, during this period, returned each evening to our muddy berth in the oily waters just above the old Transporter Bridge in the town. That this river might possess a wild beauty of its own, let alone be a fine trout-fishing water, completely eluded me. It was confirmed in my mind as a disaster, like the Mersey. It was to be another thirty years, when I returned to work in the region, before my eyes were opened to its true nature—a river of great distinction, whose course, as it matures from the boundless energies of youth, and through the growing experiences of age, reveals a wide variety of character and a rich diversity of wild life.

From its source the Tees, 2,000 feet up on the Pennines, is a typical mountain beck, whose eager hurry is only arrested as it enters the splendid reservoir of Cow Green. Then, shortly after it emerges from the confines of the dam, it celebrates a regained freedom by plunging in a milk-white torrent almost 200 feet down the majestic cataract of Cauldron Snout. From here to High Force, the highest waterfall in England, it continues its heedless, heady way through a valley, the flanks of which rise to high scars, formed when the ice-age yielded. At this stage it marches with the famous Pennine Way, and weary hikers pause beside its rocks to take refreshment, and, perhaps, search for fossils. High Force marks the final, carefree fling of youth.

After this extravagance, the river starts to widen gradually, its flow grows steadier and more purposeful, developing in a series of white water shallows, longer glides and deeper pools that wind in and out of rock-hewn gorges and between steep banks, now lined with trees, into gentle meadowlands. The upper reaches down to High Force are the sole preserve of trout but, below this point, the trout share the river with the graceful grayling, and coarse fish become more plentiful as the river descends; below Croft-on-Tees the waters are chiefly of interest to coarse anglers, and the tidal waters reach as far as Worsall.

The real triumph of the Tees, however, in recent years has been the successful return of both salmon and sea-trout. In earlier years it had been a noted salmon river, but increasing pollution at the mouth had reduced the oxygen levels to the point where the runs had ceased completely. The reversal came partly as a result of the growing recession, but mainly through the determined efforts of locally-based industries and the authorities to clean the river. On my last visit to fish there I saw a magnificent salmon showing some few hundred yards below Broken Scar to the south west of Darlington; a coarse fisherman had, in fact, hooked this one on a maggot, but was quite unable to hold him for more than a few seconds. The first rod-caught salmon in season was landed in 1982 after an interval of forty-five long years, and the runs have improved steadily ever since.

Fishings on the Tees are mostly in the hands of local angling associations with a few privately-owned parts here and there; the upper river belongs to two large estates, each owning one bank, and day and season permits are readily obtainable from either. It was, however, the luck of a chance encounter that for two consecutive seasons provided me with a week's fishing on a two-mile private stretch above Piercebridge, which proved some of the finest river-trouting I have enjoyed anywhere.

The old lady, now widowed for many years, who had given me permission to fish this water, lived alone save for a butler and, at this stage in her life, a resident nurse, in a large and somewhat crumbling mansion overlooking the river. She had been a noted sports-woman in her day, both as a shot and a salmon fisher, and, though past eighty, was planning to fish for salmon in Scotland that very summer. One evening, when I called on her to leave some trout, she told me the exact number of salmon she had bagged in her career and it was well over the thousand. It was sad that she died just about the time the salmon were beginning to return to her river.

It had never been the custom of the hall to issue fishing permits to the general public, who could not be relied upon to respect the country code, and there was no means of supervising them or their fishing methods. She had, however, made an exception in favour of the local police and fire brigade because, as she explained to me, they were the people who looked after you. I was very privileged to have been given permission to fish there, due entirely to the fact that my wife was one of the few nurses looking after her whom she really liked. New waters are always exciting and, since the butler had told me that the police and fire permits were seldom used, they were apparently only lightly fished.

It was Easter holiday fishing on both occasions and only two or three weeks into the season, a time of year when the waters of the upper river, at 1,200 feet, would still have been too cold. Leaving my car in the courtyard of the hall, I made my way through the corner of a wood, loudly scolded by a company of rooks, busy at their nests in the tops of the tall trees. Anemone and sorrell carpeted the woodland floor in white with pale primrose and bright celandine-like stars on the milky way. Already the buds on the trees were showing green and, through the din of rooks, the notes of a chiffchaff heralded a new beginning. As I arrived at the more sheltered reaches of the mid-river, I could feel the warmth of the early sun, and the evidence of spring was all about me.

The first outings of each new season are charged with an emotional quality that is peculiarly their own. The extravagances of high summer are yet to come, but now, under the surge and thrust of life that is awakening on every quarter, winter's citadel lies stormed and fallen, releasing the hostage spirit to share again the joys of a remembered freedom. Just to be standing beside a trout river in the spring of the year and to feel the fly-rod in the hand seems to alter the whole chemistry of the body, as every nerve is tightened, every action quickened and the whole frame trembles in sharp anticipation. Too long has the rod lain in its winter sheaf.

The river was large and open enough for me to start with a team of three wet-flies to be fished across and down the stream, and I put up a March Brown, Greenwell's Glory and Black Zulu, a choice which, as things turned out, I had little reason to reconsider. Most of my trout-fishing on the wide, spate rivers is across and down, although on narrower rivers I always prefer to work upstream, fishing the flies just beneath the surface. Then, at the first signs of a hatch of fly and rising fish, I invariably change to the single dry-fly.

On this morning there were no such signs of fly life when I started, but I was hoping to see the olives later, any time after midday. By about 1.30 pm I had reached a small pebbled island, which divided the stream, and there in front of me, in a fastish run beneath an overhanging bough of beech, I saw the first trout break surface. I could see now that the large dark olives were on the water, riding the crest of the stream in all their ethereal beauty. The sight of a first trout rise each year is a moment of pure magic, an annual assurance, if such be needed, that God is in His heaven and all is well.

At this time of year the hatch was unlikely to last long, so I changed quickly to a dry Olive and, kneeling on the pebbles, sidecast to land my fly near the head of the run. The current, however, was flecking the water with white wisps of foam, and this caused me to lose sight of the fly, with the result that, when the trout came, I was much too late on him, and he refused any subsequent offers. The fellow beneath the beech branch was the one to try for now, and I judged that the fly would just about reach him before the line straightened and began to drag. He turned out to be the first of three I took from that pool during the thirty-five minutes that the olive hatch lasted.

Dry-fly on the river is for me the most attractive form of fishing that I know, with so many different ingredients: it calls for nice calculations of approach, stance and distance as well as appreciation of all the delicate nuances that there are in the flow of the stream. Drag on the fly is the problem that must be avoided at all costs. Wet-fly, after all, is random fishing with the flies searching large areas of water, and, if carried out systematically, they will eventually cover fish. In contrast the dry-fly is always specific, for now the hunter pursues a sighted quarry, which means that, if he falls short in any aspect of the chase, whether in the stalking or the execution of his art, that quarry will go free. The trout only rises where he wants to rise and never where you would like him to rise, which gives him the initiative. The best trout tend to lie at the edges of the main current, rather than directly in it and, if, as is often the case, they are rising on the far bank, one has to work out how to enable the fly to cover them before the stream starts to belly the line and cause the inevitable and fatal drag. In virtually all these instances the fly will only be actually fishing for one or two seconds at the most.

In order to avoid the leader coming over the fish's window of vision I normally try to cast my fly either obliquely up-river or straight across the river, though in places the strength of the stream may be sufficient to conceal the nylon. On rivers like the Tees, however, there are several pools—where, for instance, it passes through a gorge—that demand a downstream dry-fly. Concealment is even more vital now, and the fly must land on a loose line so that the current may carry it to the fish before the line finally straightens. The strike too must be delayed fractionally longer to allow the fish to turn with the fly, otherwise one will be pulling it straight out of his mouth.

My delight on these spring mornings was enhanced, as ever, and shared in full measure by the water birds. Wading ashore to find a spot for lunch, I flushed a solitary woodcock which sprang up from the undergrowth with a great clatter, and, then, as I looked above me into the patterns of fast-ripening buds, I spotted the goosander, perched high in a tree and clearly regarding me with deep suspicion. Wigeon and mallard were also on the river and dippers seldom out of sight, but I missed the bright blaze of a passing kingfisher. That winter had been exceptionally severe and many would not have survived it. Further downstream, a mink swam at leisure the whole width of the river, not many yards in front of where my flies were fishing.

On the eleven days that I had on this stretch I caught fifty-five sizeable trout at an average weight of just under three quarters of a pound; all three flies had contributed, with the Black Zulu on the tail accounting for the two largest at $1\frac{1}{4}$lbs each. Despite it being so early in the season, the fish were all in excellent condition and two that I caught still had the half-digested frames of stone loach protruding from their gullets. For much of its length the Tees runs over limestone, which makes for good feeding, and minnows and bullheads (or miller's thumbs) are also present as well as some crayfish, so too are the juicy creeper nymphs of the large stonefly.

Later on in the season the top waters will provide exhilarating fishing, energetic days that are full of the rewards of their own distinctive interest, but it is a different world entirely. Here one operates in open country on a mountain torrent that bounds its way through the sparser pastures of scattered hill farms, divided by walls of stone, against a back-drop of high, craggy fells. Crows hunt for carrion, rabbits scurry and sheep and shaggy highland cattle graze the rough grasses.

Fishing methods will also change, for this is the ideal water to be fishing two small wet-flies upstream on a short line. Favoured patterns are the Partridge and Orange and the Snipe and Purple, both well-loved flies on the northern rivers, and rightly so, even though I may feel only half-dressed without my Greenwell's Glory on the end. The Snipe and Yellow can be an effective pattern on some days and, if the fish are reluctant to take on top, a lightly-weighted nymph will usually succeed. A longish rod—ten or eleven feet— can also prove an added advantage, allowing the flies to search thoroughly around and over and between the rocks, as they work this way and that under the vagaries of the stream's flow. The trout usually break surface when they take, but the eyes must always be alert for that gleam of gold, as one turns on the fly beneath the water, and, once hooked, they play like tigers in these rapids, running the line around the boulders and often into the pool below. There are plenty of half pounders in this section of the river with a pound fish always a possibility. For me this type of wet-fly fishing runs a very close second to the dry-fly; the casting arm will have more work to do in the upstream wet-fly, but both call for the same intensity of concentration.

Of the smaller birds to cheer you on the upland river will be sandpipers, dippers, wagtails and the pied flycatcher, but the one you take to be a blackbird will probably turn out to be a ring ouzel—he's like a blackbird in a parson's collar. Fishing a pool up there one fine May day I again noticed the olives hatching, only more abundantly this time, and a pair of pied flycatchers were busily engaged feeding young in their nest in the junipers behind me. I remember thinking then that, what with the hungry trout below me and the hard-pressed flycatchers above me, who would be an olive spinner? The life of a river fly cannot be all that much fun. Most of it is spent in the dark, dismal depths of the water, with the rapture of their love dance in the scented summer's air but a fleeting moment only, and at every stage of their existence from egg to nymph or caddis, dun and spinner, they are a prime source of food for hungry creatures; even after death the spent bodies of the female spinners as they float spreadeagled on the river, their ovipositing accomplished, are eagerly accepted by voracious trout.

What really makes the day, however, will be a rare and lovely flower that has become almost the emblem of Upper Teesdale. This is the spring gentian, an alpine plant of intense and brilliant blue, with single flowers, two inches high, set on rosettes of light green leaves. The only other place I know where it grows wild is on the Burren in the County Clare.

Autumn finds me back on the middle Tees again, the quarry now being the quick-rising grayling. Iron blue duns will be hatching on the river and the imitation, fished on top will give the cream of the fishing. The year has almost come full cycle. The boughs that at Easter were burgeoning with spring are now afire with yellow, gold, russet and red leaves. The first frosts will soon bring them tumbling and spinning to be carried on the waters. The light fades early on a late autumn's afternoon, an eerie mist begins to lift off the river, bringing a distinct chill that presages the oncoming winter, the tawny owls start to call. As I wade ashore, my eye just catches a streak of flame-tipped azure, and I know that the kingfisher is home once more. My fingers may be numb, but my heart will be warmed by the thought that the salmon and sea-trout, and now the kingfisher, are all back where they belong.

My homeward drive brings me into Middlesbrough, and I cross the river once more, carried, for old time's sake, by that grand old lady—the Transporter Bridge. She creaks and groans as she always did: the bright grayling pools, where I have spent my day, have grown dark and sluggish, reflecting now the neon-glow of the night-time city, her commerce stilled: the first berth of my beloved gunboat is occupied by the Port Authority's fireboat. The noble river, the Transporter and I have all grown older, like the year itself.

Up in the dales, above the rivers, a group of six reservoirs lie in open moorland country, and all in fairly close proximity, their names are Balderhead, Blackton and Hury (in Baldersdale), Grassholm and Selset (in Lunedale) and the queen of them all, as well as the highest, Cow Green (in Teesdale). Taken overall, the average number of rod days per season is high, which is hardly surprising for, although situated in wild country, none of them is much more than fifty miles from large concentrations of population, and in today's terms fifty miles or so is nothing for a good day's fishing. They are all managed by the Northumbrian Water Authority, who pursue a very enlightened policy, which caters admirably for the diverse requirements of modern trout-fishers. Grassholm and Hury are run as straightforward 'put and take' fisheries, regularly stocked with brown and rainbow trout throughout the season, and between them these two attract the vast majority of rods, thereby absorbing most of the pressure on the fishings.

The other four are deliberately left unstocked so that, apart from their dams, they have all the characteristics of truly wild waters as well as possessing the ability to show a good head of naturally-bred trout each year. Truly wild stillwaters with the capacity to breed large trout are an ever-diminishing resource in our land, which makes it all the more encouraging to find an Authority that not only recognises the intrinsic and spiritual value that such waters have for fishermen, but is also even prepared to sacrifice revenue in order to provide and preserve them in a natural state.

I have fished these stillwaters more than 150 times, often staying overnight at local farms or hostelries, and my diaries still bring back the triumphs and disasters as well as the enchantment of so many days when I would cover miles of open water, in fair weather and storm, and always with the prospect of sport with these wild trout of the hills. They have always been my preference and I concentrated mainly on the three waters of Cow Green, Balderhead and Selset. I remember coming off a mountain on the west of Ireland after a long day's climbing and fishing a distant lough, and calling at an isolated lounge-bar with the thirst of the devil on me. I soon got talking to a local, already well into the porter. 'You from England?', he asked, as if he did not already know. 'I used to work over there meself. Grand place it was too'. The Irish like to flatter and I imagined he had probably laboured in the Midlands or around the London area, as so many of his countrymen had done. 'I was building the dam at Selset', he said. 'Well you did a grand job too', I replied. 'I was fishing on it just the other day'. Strange, that within a week I should meet, quite by chance on a far Hibernian shore, a fellow who had actually worked on the construction. What I did not tell him was that his dam had nearly cost me my life earlier on in the year.

I suppose that every fisherman suffers the nemesis of falling in a few times in the course of his career. On this occasion I was fishing off the dam in early April on a day when a bitter east wind was blowing straight from the Siberian steppes. The dam sloped gently down to the water in a series of heavy slabs of masonry, perfectly safe to fish from except for about 2 feet from the water's edge, where the slabs were covered in green weed; I knew quite well that if one trod there one would be stepping into the realms of no-return. Because of the cold I was wearing mittens but, even so, the exposed fingers soon began to numb and turn white. Nothing moved for a long time, and then quite suddenly, and against all expectations, I was into a fish. If it did nothing to restore my circulation it certainly warmed my spirits, kindling a fresh enthusiasm that bordered on the careless. Shortly, my front foot strayed onto the fatal green, and I found myself sliding slowly, but irrevocably, into the fast-deepening waters. It is said that in such circumstances the kaleidoscope of one's life flashes before the mind's eye. In my case that did not happen but, with the right hand holding the rod up, the left struggled to wedge senseless fingers into any gap there might be between the slabs.

It was not the first, or even the second, time that I have fallen in, and I had learnt long ago to keep what I call my survival kit—a complete change of clothes plus a towel—always in the back of my Morris Traveller throughout the season. A quick dash now to the fishing hut for a rub-down and change of clothing, then back to the 'Rose and Crown' at Mickleton, where I was staying, to deposit wet garments, sink a whisky and borrow a pair of wellington boots from Mr and Mrs Lynch, the landlords, and in less than an hour I was back on Selset for six more fish. I mentioned my escapade to Geoff Sage, one of the bailiffs, whom I met the next day, and he informed me that the water temperature was 36 degrees F!

It is surprising how one can take fish in such cold weather. Five years before I had been on the much higher lake, Cow Green this time, which stands at 1600 feet, again in the first week of April, when a sudden snow-blizzard descended, making it necessary for me to free the line that had frozen to the rod-rings before each cast, and I still managed to take three lusty trout. I am not a natural masochist and confess that such endurance fishing has little pleasure to it—I now prefer to leave Cow Green alone until May has come.

I do not know how this lake acquired the charming name of Cow Green but it really is a total misnomer, suggesting gentle cattle meadows, whereas it lies on rugged heather moorland where the 'Go-Bak, Go-Bak' cry of the red grouse fills the air, proclaiming his sovereign territorial rights in a barren landscape. Here too are curlew, snipe, redshank, lapwing, golden plover, sandpipers and a variety of duck as well as large concentrations of black headed gulls which nest on the shoreline. Rising above the lake are some of the finest grouse moors in Britain, well-keepered and providing heavy returns to the guns each season.

The decision to dam the Tees and create the lake caused much heated controversy at the time, because it involved the flooding of a unique area of herb-rich grassland, which overlay a coarse and granulated limestone (sugar limestone) and contained rare alpine plants. It ended only when the conservation interests were carefully heeded and the continued existence of the plants assured. Also, now submerged, are the old mine-workings, where once a hardy breed of miners had earned a livelihood excavating lead ore and barium sulphate. Up to the coming of the flood, a pair of ring ouzels had built their nest each year in one of the mineshaft entrances. The end result was to provide a lake of exceptional rugged beauty, part of whose five and a quarter mile shore is restricted as a nature reserve.

Its undoubted value as a fishery is due to the superb quality of the trout that it produces, something which the Freshwater Biological Association in Windermere has carefully monitored over the years through a comprehensive policy of tagging. Anglers who catch tagged fish are requested to return the tags to the laboratories, together with some scales from below the dorsal fin, as well as giving details of its length, place and date of capture. Tag return forms for this purpose are supplied in the fishing hut, so that anglers can fill them in and post them when they enter their own catch on the sheet at the end of the day. Nor is this information for the boffins only, for in due course each tag returned is acknowledged, showing the date the fish was tagged and its length at the time. This again is yet another example of a thoroughly enlightened approach, for it allows interested anglers, and there are many, to keep their own records of the trout that they have caught.

The limestone base would in any case suggest good feeding and the tag returns confirm a very encouraging growth rate, which, coupled with excellent spawning facilities, both in the top river and the many 'sikes' around the shoreline, makes Cow Green the jewel it is.

The lakes are all different, each one possessing its own characteristics and wild life as well as its favoured bays and corners; Balderhead has all the ruggedness of Cow Green, treeless, save for a cluster of blasted stumps, and with some very steep sides where tiny rivulets drop their waters in a last cascade that sends ripples into the lake. Sheltering in one of these to enjoy my bait out of the wind, I noticed a small rise 100 feet below me, and, depositing a half-eaten sandwich, I quit my precarious perch to make my way down to the stream. I removed the team of wet flies and substituted a single dry Black Gnat, and within twenty minutes managed to quadruple my morning's achievement, taking four trout to it, whilst across the waters the 'honk' of a pair of Canada geese told me that once again they were busy raising a family.

The enjoyment of birds and animals has always marched closely alongside my fishing expeditions, and I keep my eyes and ears alert for certain species on particular waters. Once at the head of Cow Green I remember freezing motionless as I spotted an otter, quite oblivious of me, swimming in the water no more than fifty yards from where I was standing, and I watched him for several minutes before he became alarmed and disappeared towards the river. For me, the most fascinating of all are the raptors—the eagles, falcons, hawks and owls—swift, powerful killers of the air, which long ages of evolution have fashioned so superbly for the task. Alone and watchful, they stalk the wide skies with a noble elegance and economy of movement that is the quintessence of all hunting technique and, following my own recreation, I feel a distant kinship with them. Selset is the territory of the short-eared owl and, as I make my way along the shore, he quarters the hillside behind me with slow, measured flight, searching for the field voles which scurry amongst tussocks of rough grasses. He was hunting with me on the final day of the 1980 season when I caught on a Wickham's Fancy the best trout of that year to come off Selset.

I also used to bring youngsters to these lakes to introduce them to the joys of fly-fishing. Peter Appleby—better known as 'Apples'—was fifteen when I first brought him to Cow Green. Since those years he has become the best allround fly-fisherman that I know and we still fish together when circumstances allow. He now earns his living on the Durham coalface, hewing the black gold from seams that lie seven miles out under the North Sea. Few can value more than he, working as he does in the dark, dank bowels of the earth, the release and freedom which the great skies and sweeps of the dales and the bright rivers, which they spawn, afford the spirit, a birthright that we share with so many lovely creatures.

Chapter 4

Fly-Fishing the Sea

After the war I worked for twelve years in a bustling Boys' Club in the Everton area of Liverpool, where the streets still bore heavy scars from the German blitz, though its spirit remained unbowed, its people proud and confident and fiercely jealous of their heritage in a noble city. Our club year reached its climax with the ending of the summer camp, and by this time both mind and body stood in need of a recharge. Soon, the football crowds would be thronging through the Anfield turnstiles, and the famous Kop would be ringing once again to the strains of 'You'll never walk alone', but that was precisely what I now needed to do: it was time to quit the unremitting city and, in the words of the psalmist, 'to seek refreshment in the multitude of peace'.

My eyes would turn once more to the far off, lonely places, where wild seabirds cried and wide waters gave back the brightness of huge skies. August is not the best of months to fish for brown trout, unless it be on upland waters, but it is a splendid time of year to hunt the silver sea-trout, and where better than the distant Isles of Shetland?

I left Liverpool on the night train bound for the grey, granite town of Aberdeen where the harvest of the North Sea was landed daily. From here, my plane took off from Dyce Airport into a clear sky and soon I was looking down on the rugged patchwork of the Scottish Highlands, then the open sea before the Orkneys lay below. Further still and we crossed the little Fair Isle, halfway between Orkney and Shetland. It stood out very lonely in the vastness of ocean, its sea-sculpted coastline flecked with white spume. Now owned by the National Trust, it still nurtures a small population as well as an important bird observatory. Each year fieldfares, redwings, wheatears, siskins, bramblings, crossbills, pipits, puffins and rarer birds, too, are caught and ringed here.

The isle, only three miles in length, is probably best known for its famous knitwear pattern. Today, its two extremities are marked by lighthouses but, in earlier years, its storm-tossed shores claimed many victims. Some have suggested that the Fair

Isle design was brought by Spanish sailors wrecked in the Armada. One such vessel certainly did ground there on the night of August 17th, 1588, having had the worst of a brush with Lord Howard of Effingham's fleet in the English Channel. The two hundred or so sailors who made the shore killed and ate everything in sight, and soon threatened the locals with starvation. The islanders found a remedy by pushing some over the cliffs and shipping the rest to the Shetlands, where they were more kindly treated.

The Shetland archipelago contains a string of islands nearly seventy miles in length and twenty across at the widest point. The mainland itself is shaped like the figure nine and tapers in a long, southern peninsula to Sumburgh Head. Here, a brief patch of level ground affords a bleak and windswept airfield. The islands lie halfway between London and the Arctic Circle and mostly north of the sixtieth parallel, buffeted on one side by the North Atlantic and by the North Sea on the other. Yet for all this they enjoy a very decent climate. The air, being warmed by that extension of the Gulf Stream called the North Atlantic Drift, never gets very cold. Less favourable are the fierce gales which frequently sweep the land, and these, together with a poor soil, are the reasons why trees are such a rarity. The first impression is one of barrenness, but tiny fields and neat, bright crofts soon soften this appearance.

The Shetlanders themselves are exceedingly friendly people, very open and quick to make a stranger feel at home amongst them. They are highly industrious and strongly independent in their outlook. Proud of their Norse heritage, they have never regarded themselves as an appendage to Scotland. Their annual festival of 'Up Helly Aa', which takes place on the last Tuesday in January in the capital of Lerwick, is a vivid proclamation, both of their heroic past and of their Viking ancestry. Its roots lie in a pagan fire festival, celebrating the end of the winter solstice and the rebirth of the sun. In earlier years, it sometimes got out of hand as flaming tar-barrels were rolled through the narrow alleys of the town.

Though more controlled today, it is still performed with the same gusto, reaching its dramatic climax with the burning of a Viking galley. These sturdy folk live partly off the land, but mainly from the treacherous seas that wash their shores. The long centuries have bred a race of superb seamen, and the casual visitor who comes amongst them to catch fish is with friends from the start.

The airport bus left me in Lerwick, from where I took a taxi to the Bridge of Walls, a tiny settlement in the heart of the western peninsula. This ride gave me my first insight into the reason why this is such a paradise for the sea-trout fisherman. It is as if whoever made the land deliberately set out to create an impossible jigsaw. The entire coastline is fretted and fragmented by long, narrow sea inlets, known here as voes, which resemble in miniature the fiords of Norway. The longer of these voes divide further into smaller ones, which in turn are fed from the land by peat-black burns with quivering banks, which issue out of inland lochs. To walk the whole shoreline of the main island would be a mammoth undertaking. The entire western strip is a watery mazeland where the whimbrel and curlew, golden plover and wheatear inhabit wide vacancies. Shrouded in mist or swept by rains, it can be desolate, but beneath clear skies it has all the beauty of a virginal landscape, almost untouched by man.

The sea-trout start to gather in these voes in March and April and continue to do so throughout the summer. By late August and September they are joined by large shoals of the smaller sort, around a pound in weight and variously known as herling or finnock. All move up and down the voes with the tides, as they await the rains which, draining the sour hillsides, swell the burns. These now afford them easy passage to the fresh water and the spawning grounds of the feeder streams. Only a few hours' rain will raise the levels sufficiently. If, however, the weather remains dry, and only light rain has fallen, large numbers of fish remain in the voes to nose around the inlets when the tide is full. Their lines of movement within the voes vary from place to place, but in the main they seem to keep close to the shoreline.

49

So numerous are these voes that there are at least forty different places in the islands where sea-trout can be fished for and caught: it would need a lifetime to explore them all thoroughly. There are estuaries in other countries where sea-trout can be taken on the fly, but what makes the Shetlands unique is the sheer abundance of it all. The holiday angler has to rely on local knowledge, always readily given here, as well as the evidence of his own eyes. Though plentiful, these fine fish are by no means easy to catch—as I was soon to discover.

I stayed at the Bridge of Walls, and what I found here was typical of many similar places in the Shetlands. The main road, that ran across the centre of the peninsula, crossed a bridge at the head of the Voe of Browland, itself the northern arm of the larger Gruting Voe. At the bridge the voe narrowed into shallow water, broken here and there by rocks and then opened up above to form Brouster Loch, which contained brackish water and was fed by the tides. At its head a narrow, canal-like burn, with a sluice gate across it, connected with the Upper Loch of Brouster, now freshwater. The sea-trout will pass quite easily from the voe into the lower loch on the spring tides, but they seem to prefer to wait for a freshet of rain to raise the levels. A combination of these two would bring many fish up.

Close to the bridge, Mr and Mrs Hobbin ran a guest-house, less than a stone's throw from the water's edge, which they combined with the running of the local post office. I stayed here and found it a homely place, very comfortable and with good plain food. My three or four fellow guests were, not surprisingly, also fishermen. When the day's sport was over, we gathered round the fire, dissecting the day's events and listening to improbable tales. Mr Hobbin, like many another Shetlander, had been on several whaling expeditions and always had a fund of good stories to tell.

At the start of my stay it was clear that the voe was full of sea-trout and they were also present in good numbers in the lower loch, but very few seemed to be up as yet in the freshwater loch above. By the end of August, the situation was still very much the same, and we decided to try and induce an artificial spate by means of the sluice gate in the burn. The following day we closed this down in order to build up a head of water, intending to let it go forty-eight hours later. Unfortunately, I missed the end of this experiment as I was then on my way back to Merseyside. A subsequent letter from my colleagues, however, informed me that, having let this water go, they had later enjoyed good sport in the upper loch. Many fish had clearly been stimulated to make the passage of the burn.

In view of these continuing low levels, most of my fishing had to be confined to the voe itself, the small sea pool below the bridge and the brackish, lower loch. The voe could be fished either in waders from the shore or else from the Hobbin's boat, but the boat was much the better bet. The waving tangles of seaweed that grew close by the shore made wading decidedly chancy, and one careless step would have left you floundering amongst the crabs. It also severely restricted the amount of water one could cover. I watched one fellow in brogued chest-waders who was wielding a double-handed salmon rod—grilse were also running in the voe—but I never saw him connect. The boat gave far more scope, as well as the chance of playing a fish in open ground.

The incoming tide is always the one to fish and the best times are one hour after the flood begins to an hour before high water. Having been reared on the small mountain streams, I found it very strange at first to be fly-fishing the sea. In the vastness of my surroundings the little fly seemed absurdly small, and I guessed that to flog the water at random would be a complete waste of time and energy. This is the point where local knowledge became vital. In Browland Voe the sea-trout followed the shoreline pretty closely, quite often betraying their presence by plunging and breaking surface in a kind of wild, unorchestrated ballet of the sea. Probably this happened as they chased small fry to the top on the fringes of the weed.

One evening, as I was lying off in the boat with a single Bloody

Butcher on my cast, and scanning the shoreline for those tell-tale signs that I knew would send my pulses racing, I became aware, in the strange way that one does, that I too was being watched. My fellow anglers were standing on the little jetty in front of the guest-house, and I noticed at least one pair of binoculars with them. If I was going to make a hash of things, I would rather do it alone. On the other hand, if I was about to perform well, they were welcome to watch and learn something from a master at his craft! They were soon to have their fun and so was I.

Fifty or so yards to seaward, I saw the signs I had been waiting for—the sea-trout were moving up the voe. As quietly as I could, I manoeuvred the boat so as to intercept them; and waited my time. Then, as a sporting gun will follow through a crossing pheasant in the field, I deliberately aimed off, landing my fly well in front of the splashing fish. I cast a second time and then again. At the next, the fly was seized mightily; this was no pluck of an interested trout, but a real bang of a take which bent the whole rod. Three spectacular leaps in quick succession showed a fine fish, bright as a burnished bar of steel. Was this to be my first sea-trout from the sea? I tried to steady him, but to no avail. He had his own ideas, and my reel began to sing as he powered away, using all the muscle of his good sea-feeding. He knew precisely where to go—straight for the tangle weed by the water's edge. I increased the pressure, desperate now to stem this rush, and hopeful of turning him, but it was not to be. The rod straightened and my fly came back. Within ten minutes I had hooked and lost another three! Such can be the speed of this seawater fishing, once the shoals have been located, tremendously exciting and calling for both steadiness and concentration.

When I finally tied the boat up at the jetty it contained one fish only out of a possible eight or nine, but my first evening in the voe had provided plenty of entertainment all round, definitely high on sport if low on achievement. In fact, it set the pattern for much of the holiday—with many more fish being hooked than ever came near the net. What I had not fully reckoned with was the very soft and tender nature of a sea-trout's mouth when in sea water. I imagine the reason for this is the fact that they are still actively feeding at this time and, therefore, a fairly sensitive mouth is needed. The transition from life in saltwater to life in freshwater is accompanied by several chemical changes in their metabolism, and, as feeding ceases, so their mouths grow firmer. They seemed to spend quite lengthy periods in the brackish loch, which they probably found to be a convenient staging post whilst acclimatising to the new conditions, and even here the hookholds were never really secure. It is for this reason that one has to play them far more gently than those which have been up for some time.

Once hooked, a fish usually boils on the surface before beginning his display of aerobatics. This is the first critical period. Some may disagree, but I am a firm believer in the necessity for lowering the rod-tip each time he jumps clear, for, once allowed to fall back on a taut line, the chances are that the hook will pull out. In the next phase he will motor for the weeds if possible and, when this happens, he should be allowed his head. Many are heavy fish and, provided one is fishing a single fly only, they can plough through the weeds without entangling the tackle. The attempt to try and stem this run is more than likely to end in disaster. This had been my error. To win, one has to gamble and take risks. Fishing in the voes of Shetland is not for the nervous, for, in these clear northern waters, one can often see the fish and follow his every movement.

My colleagues on the jetty had thoroughly enjoyed the evening's pantomine and, as we gathered round the supper table, I rode their ribald comments with ease and all the aplomb of a true authority, endeavouring to illustrate his lessons for the benefit of dull pupils!

Sea-trout are capricious creatures and seldom behave the same way two days running. The small sea pool below the bridge was always alive with fish towards high water, and one could stand and cast at them for half an hour without moving anything. Then, just as one was least expecting it, a fish would strike. It is this very unpredictability that is, perhaps, the hallmark of sea-trout fishing as well as one of its enduring fascinations.

The angler who goes down to the voes, determined to make a heavy bag, will vary his tactics and will probably carry a spinning rod as well. A favourite local bait is a strip of fresh-caught mackerel, with which the voes teemed in August. Old Jamie, who lived with his wife above the Hobbin's, never went down for 'a troot' without first catching a few of them. This bait, which resembles a sand-eel—always a favourite food item—is either spun slowly or fished with a fly-rod, mounted on Stewart tackle; bags of a score or more are not uncommon. Spinning, however, does not attract me, nor do I say this out of any sense of superiority. I just find it too mechanical and lacking in touch to be satisfying, but there is certainly no denying the skill of the good spinners. I much preferred to stay with the fly even if the fish did not.

The many lochs of Shetland also offered pleasant brown trout fishing. On most of them one could catch half-pounders from the shoreline, and native wild fish all of them. Some of these waters held larger fish—Danny's Loch, within walking distance of the Bridge of Walls, was one of them, and here one could find beautiful trout of a pound or more. One afternoon, I rowed the boat down the voe for about one and a half miles and beached it near the end of a south-pointing peninsula, where I pulled it well up onto the shore, and then climbed the hillside to look for the Loch of Grunavoe. I knew it was not a sea-trout water but I had come, in a lazy frame of mind, to enjoy the warm and sunny afternoon, and to see what I could do with the brownies. The loch, when I found it, lay in a small hollow at the centre of the plateau, where it sparkled like a bright ring of light on a last finger of land, as it reached out for the sea.

It was a lonely place and, as far as the eye could see in all directions, without any traces of human habitation or endeavour. From the days when the longships had come, and wild sea-adventurers had roamed the land, it would scarcely have changed at all—perhaps those fierce northmen too had paused from their plunder to find refreshment beside this shining ring of water. I put up my rod and was soon starting to catch a few trout, but, after the exertions of rowing and climbing and with the throb of Merseyside still beating in my head, I laid my rod against a rock and settled down to absorb the timeless landscape that now enfolded me.

What was to etch the name of Grunavoe so firmly on my mind, however, was neither the scenery nor the fishing, but two other happenings, both of them strange and very diverse in character: in fact so opposite were they that I remember them now only as Peace and War.

One of them, as I was to discover later, had a perfectly rational explanation, but the other transcended altogether the normal ways of the world as I knew them.

The only way I can describe the first occurrence is to say that I received a visitation from the spirits, of such power that I became overwhelmed by a serenity and feeling of well-being that I had never known before or since. Those who indulge in drugs and artificial stimulants speak of 'going on a trip' or 'being on a high', but these self-induced forms of rapture carry with them the scent of death, and the return journey seems almost always to lead into a pit of despair. My visitation, if such it was, was essentially life-giving, abounding with light and joy, with all earthly shackles loosed and fallen away. If what I was granted beside the bright water on the high plateau was some kind of foretaste of what it may be like, when the rods are put away for good and we ourselves cross that final bourn into the realms beyond time, then it will not be bad at all.

It is told of Handel that, when he had finished composing the Hallelujah Chorus, he turned to a friend, with tears on his face, and said 'I saw all heaven before my eyes'. Now, if great music and inspired literature can move our spirits, so too can the associations of place. I have long known, since those formative days when I wandered, lonely with my thoughts and at leisure, beside the mountain stream, that the business of fishing was bound in with the spirit of place. Angling, in its many forms, leads us all to a place of waters—it may be a tide-washed, rockbound creek, a loch tucked secretly beneath the clouds, or a favourite glide, where the river curls gently and lazy chub feed, at ease, under trailing arms of willow. Water is the elemental source, from which life came and by which it is sustained, the place where unseen powers still hold their carnival, and dance to a music that cleanses our minds and frees our spirits from the toils of the world.

The peace that had so engrossed me proved to be short-lived, and was about to be rudely shattered as I found myself the object of a violent attack. My mistake had been to imagine that I had this airy plateau to myself. When it happened, I had resumed my fishing and was picking my steps across the boulders, casting away happily and minding my own business. The unseen assailant came suddenly, without warning and at great speed, out of a clear sky. In the instant before he struck I heard the thunder of wings as the air parted behind me, and then a gigantic bird came screaming over my head, ruffling my hair as it passed. The momentum of this dive took him (or probably her), three quarters of the way across the loch, where he started to bank and climb steeply before coming in again on a frontal assault this time. The whole performance lasted some ten minutes, each dive carried out with the same precision. I must have been standing too close to its chick, but so well was it camouflaged amongst the stones that I never discovered it. Frightening it may have been, but it was also a superlative display of power-flight, as good a demonstration of the Stuka divebomber as one could hope to see. I was only grateful it had not been a kamikaze job!

My attacker had been none other than the great skua, known familiarly to the Shetlanders as the 'bonxie', a real scallywag of a bird if ever there was one. It is a heavily built, brown gull with a four-and-a-half-foot wingspan, superbly adapted to flight, as I had discovered, but something from a comic opera when on the ground. It lives the life of a pirate, with feeding habits that are anything but delicate—chasing and harrying other gulls, it forces them to regurgitate their latest meal, which it then dives to retrieve for itself. It will even engage the powerful gannet, hanging onto tail or wing-tip until it gives up the fish it has just swallowed. These unsavoury feeding habits put me in mind of the Frenchman who, when faced with a plate of porridge for the first time, asked 'Do I eat zis or 'as someone already eat it?'

The bonxie was, however, to lure me onto the lonely and dramatic isle of Foula where it has its largest breeding colony in the northern hemisphere. To reach this splendid island I took the postboat out of Scalloway, a small fishing port and once the Shetlands' capital, for the twenty seven mile journey westwards, and even in summer the little boat bucked and tossed in the broad Atlantic swell.

Foula is Britain's remotest inhabited island, and, although geographically a part of the Shetland archipelago, it is isolated from the main group with fourteen miles of ocean separating it from the little village of Walls, the nearest landing on the Shetland mainland to the east. In reality it stands alone, proud and aloof, far out into the Atlantic, perched high on awesome cliffs. The tallest of these is the Kame, a sheer rockface, 1,200 feet in height.

In the all-too-brief months of summer it rides at ease, flowers colour the sparse pastures under skies that become a wheeling circus of seabirds. In the winter the aspect is altogether different. Huge seas now storm the island walls, scouring far inland with their caustic breath. The gale force winds also drive against them and, becoming compressed, spill over their tops to sweep the island with an increased fury, seldom experienced elsewhere. These concentrations of wind assume a visible form, like swift, revolving mirages of heat and seem to take on an entity of their own. The island folk know them as 'flans', and everything movable is stoutly tied down at the onset of winter. The Sneug, the highest mountain, lours darkly on the west like a forbidding sentinel, its 1,373 feet peak lost in cloud.

The island is three and a half miles long by two and a half miles across and slopes down from the western side where the highest ground lies. Most of it is sour, black peat which provides the staple fuel of the islanders. A small amount of hay is harvested each year, but severe exposure allows little grain or root crop to be cultivated, though a hardy type of kale is grown. Sheep form the basis of today's crofting and find summer grazing on the hills, with hay as the sole winter feeding. The island also provides a home for a large variety of seabirds, and many of the smaller birds of passage also find it a welcome staging post to rest up on their long migration flights.

For centuries, Foula has provided a home and a way of life for a race of islanders, whose fortunes, like the tides around them, have ebbed and flowed with changing circumstances. In the past, the population has averaged around one hundred and fifty and, although visitations of the dreaded muckle fever (smallpox) have sometimes reduced it, it has managed to recover. It reached its peak at the end of the last century, when the census of 1881 showed a total population of two hundred and sixty seven with thirty three children attending the local school.

In February, 1985, Foula's population stood at forty five, with eight children attending the island primary school and five more boarding at the secondary school in Lerwick on the mainland. A hopeful sign, perhaps, is the average age of today's population, a mere thirty one, with the oldest inhabitant now an octogenarian. The last one hundred years, therefore, have seen a steady but significant decline of 83 per cent. Foula, however, has not been alone in this, a comparable depopulation having taken place throughout the Highlands and Islands.

It was fifty seven years ago this summer that His Majesty's sloop *Harebell* sailed out of Village Bay with thirty-six passengers on board and, in so doing, rang down the curtain on more than a thousand years of continuous habitation on the remote St Kilda's isle off the Outer Hebrides. Is Foula to follow in the wake of St Kilda's, are the hearths to grow cold there, the island left to the bonxies? It need not be so, and should certainly not be allowed to happen.

The fishing was accompanied by the annual harvesting of seabirds and their eggs, also common on the western Isles and their remote outliers. It is hard for us, who buy our poultry and eggs in neat packages from the supermarket shelves, to imagine what men these must have been, who lowered themselves seventy fathoms down a staked rope to gather eggs and reluctant fowl, with the wild ocean surging a further 500 feet below them. Fishing and fowling of this sort called for stout hearts, and both claimed their toll of lives. Most, though, were superb cragsmen.

Throughout this period there was much exchange with the mainland: islanders sailed from Shetland on whaling expeditions, the herring fishing and in the Merchant Navy, whilst girls left the island to work at the fish-gutting in Lerwick. Young bloods thought little of rowing fourteen miles for a spot of courting. All this traffic insured that the Foula community never became an inbred one.

The end of the fishing and fowling era signalled the start of the population decline, as the island reverted to crofting, now based on sheep. Cows were once more numerous but the pasturage was never adequate. Lambs and wool are the primary sources of income today and, from September to November, boats must leave the island regularly, ferrying them to the mainland: in a stormy Autumn—often the case—few passages can be made and the lambs are not shipped. The fact remains that Foula can never be self-supporting so long as it remains dependent upon crofts. Their prime resource lies in the surrounding seas rather than the land.

Foula's absurdity—and it is no less—is that there is no harbour there: nature failed to provide one. The island's sole landing place is at the Ham Voe at the base of the main settlement, a mere 150 yards long on the eastern side and ending in a small strip of sand, where the boats must be hauled ashore for safety, there being no shelter. A jetty was constructed here in 1914. Sheila Gear, who with her husband and family is one of the island's crofters, says in her book *Foula Island West of the Sun*, 'Many an islander in his daydreams has excavated out a harbour—the answer to all his problems'.

Remoteness is not experienced by the islanders in the sense of feeling isolated, though, without a harbour, they are severely cut off in adverse weather. The nearest they ever come to loneliness is when the birds depart at the end of the summer. They do, however, suffer from the remoteness of the administrative centre. Mainlanders can ring the Council and visit the town hall: they are in constant touch and can consult and attend meetings as no islander can ever do. The good people of Foula, relatively deprived as they are, are fully aware that the cost per head of providing any services for them far exceeds that on the mainland, and, for this reason, are reluctant to press their own case or push for more.

St Kilda finally died because the people's will to stay had died. This is far from the case on Foula, whose inhabitants, including their exiled young, love and cherish the island home with a fierce devotion, inherited from generations of their forebears. They are a people possessed of a naturally conservative and sturdily independent spirit, which is partly instanced by their refusal to convert from the Julian to the Gregorian calendar when the rest of Britain did so in the mid-eighteenth century; they still keep their Christmas festival on January 6th, and for them New Year begins on January 13th. Their's is a pattern of life deep-rooted in the rhythms of the seasons, the comings and going of the birds, the ebb and flow of tides. Urban-based communities have largely lost this fundamental one-ness with the land: in this respect it is they who are deprived, living, as they do, lives increasingly subsidized by artificialities. If Foula and other remote corners of the nation's land store are left to perish, then all are made the poorer, all are diminished.

I left the island full of admiration for the grit of these tenacious people who, seemingly against the odds, still clung to their comfortless, rockbound island home. At least the bonxie seemed to possess one advantage denied to them: he was protected by law, as no islanders have ever been, his future secure.

Meanwhile, on Foula they remain, as ever, a people of hope, and at long last there are now signs that a proper harbour may be becoming a reality, as opposed to what it has always been—a mere pipedream.

Chapter 5

Under the Whales' Curse

My visit to the Shetlands had apparently awakened some ancient Viking that had long lain dormant in the marrow of my being, and he was far from ready to go back to sleep, for the following year he lured me north again, this time to even more distant regions of the North Atlantic—the craggy Isles of Faroe.

I suppose that, to most people, 'Faroes' is little more than a familiar name in the regular shipping forecasts. In reality, the Faroes comprise an archipelago of twenty islands—seventeen of them inhabited—which rise almost vertically from the ocean, midway between Shetland and Iceland, at 62 degrees of northern latitude. They are volcanic in origin, constructed of basalt with a thin covering of red-brown ash that allows the steep hillsides and deep valley bottoms to be carpeted with a lush green grass, close cropped by sheep, and bright with flowers in summer. No more than 6% of the land surface however is capable of cultivation, although the remaining 94% is far from unproductive, supporting sheep and host to vast numbers of birds. The many cliff-faces and rock escarpments form nesting sites for hundreds of thousands of seabirds, as well as a temporary sanctuary for a great number of smaller birds on migration journeys. Over two hundred and fifty different species have been recorded here, and the place is an ornithologist's heaven.

At first sight, one begins to wonder that these towering rocks are inhabited at all; that they are is due more to historical and traditional factors than to economic or logical ones. The earliest recorded settlement was during the Roman occupation of Britain, when a Scottish king, together with his entourage, set sail for Northern Ireland, but, being blown off course by the winds, they made eventual landfall on the island of Sudoroy, where they founded a settlement. This had, apparently, been abandoned by the 8th century, when monks from Ireland sought for solitude on the islands, only to be disturbed by the beginning of the Viking arrivals in 825.

The birds, inhabiting, as they do, a three-dimensional world, would have had a distinct advantage over man who, confined to the horizontal plane, found it hard enough even to get ashore at all, but, wherever he managed to do so, small settlements sprang up in what shelter the land provided.

Today's population is around 44,000—the equivalent, that is, of towns like Hereford, or Scarborough—more than a quarter of whom live in the capital of Torshavn on the main island of Streymoy. This makes them the smallest of all the Scandinavian countries and, although technically belonging to the crown of Denmark, they enjoy their own autonomy, their own language, a rich national culture and a parliament which is one of the oldest in Europe. Fair hair and light blue eyes betray their Viking forebears whilst, especially on Sudoroy, the Celts still live on in the darker and more stocky frames.

Possessing this pedigree and this type of homeland, it is hardly surprising that the man of Faroes is such a magnificent seaman, as capable as he is fearless. The sea is forever around him—at no point on the islands can one stand more than 5 km from it—and he regards even his own home as though it were a ship, having a companion-way rather than a staircase. With a domestic agriculture that is only meagre, it is to the sea he looks for his own livelihood and for his country's future. His ancestors came by it and his young son's ambition will always be to embark on some unguarded boat and row it around the fiord, or into the open sea if possible; it may even claim him in the end. An island proverb refers to a boatless man as 'a man in chains'.

The sea no less dictates the climate. Because the islands lie in the drift of the Gulf Stream, they are warmer in winter than most of Britain with a mean winter temperature around 38 degrees Fahrenheit. Less favourable, though, are the many depressions which drift south westwards from Iceland, bringing storms and savage gales. The barometer can behave like a yoyo here, often moving an inch in 12 hours. Winds strike the cliff-faces to rebound with such a fury that the waterfalls, which normally cascade in long tongues of white down from the rocks that bind the mountain tops, turn about and go upwards. On several occasions, when fishing on the loch at Saksun, I was to see this weird and elemental sight, as if nature herself was out of joint, while demons danced in hues of rainbow, mocking the gale.

As I journeyed to these islands, I knew at least that I would be coming among friends, for in the war years they had been amidst the staunchest of all our allies, using their entire fishing fleet to ferry frozen fish from Iceland to our shores. Even in 1940 when the Iceland boats refused to put to sea without an air escort, which could not be provided, the Faroese continued to sail. By the spring of the following year they were landing 75% of all fish arriving at our ports. Unarmed save for a solitary bren-gun and without escort, they faced bombings, floating mines, torpedoes and, perhaps most harrowing of all, low level straffing from machine-guns, and all this as well as the cold, tempestuous seas which they were used to handling. It is a remarkable fact that, although a non-combatant power, they nevertheless sacrificed a greater proportion of men per head of population than any of the combatant powers in the process of ferrying food to our shores.

I was at school until the end of 1942 and remember clearly that, throughout the darkest years of war, the mainstay of our diet was cod from Iceland, which we believed to be completely encircled by a gigantic wall of frozen fish. With the thoughtlessness of youth, we complained bitterly about the monotony of our dinners, yet we never once went hungry. These were stirring times when young minds readily praised valour, and, if only we had known at what cost and with what indomitable courage we were privileged to eat those dinners, we would never have been so callous.

When the war was over the Faroese had lost one third of their 1939 fishing fleet—thirty-six boats in all. They were, however, to reap the rewards of their heroism, the profits were ploughed back into the industry, and today they possess the world's most modern fishing fleet. It is by far their largest industry and the huge annual catch is all processed on the islands before being exported. They have come a long way indeed since the 1870's, when the British fishing fleets went over to steam and they were able to buy the obsolete sailing vessels at a knock-down price.

My lasting impression of these islanders was of a sturdy and industrious people, who live their lives close to the heart of nature in a rain-washed homeland of savage, pristine beauty. To be fishing a lake there, as the sun breaks through to dispel the mists, bringing its ever-changing patterns of light to play upon the landscape, is to understand just why those early Viking adventurers wanted to stay and make a home there.

My outward journey was speedy enough to start with, and enabled me to enjoy my breakfast in Liverpool, morning coffee in London and lunch in Copenhagen. This kind of jet-setting, however, was hardly the right spirit in which to approach these towering rocks that lay just south of the Arctic Circle, and in any case Faroes possessed no airstrip at that time. A night spent in Copenhagen helped me to change gear mentally before embarking on a sea-passage to Torshavn, the capital of the islands. I had a forty-eight hour voyage ahead of me, which turned out rough enough to make me feel uneasy but too short to grow my sea-legs. I was decidedly unsteady as I came ashore and started to make my way towards the gaily painted, timbered houses that fronted the harbour. What I most wanted at that moment was a hotel with a hot bath, and a meal where the food stayed still on the table. What I got was completely different.

It was then, just as I was collecting my wits on the quayside, that I became aware that something unusual was about to happen. The whole township was suddenly all astir; in the general commotion people were no longer walking around, or standing in casual groups, but everyone was running here, there and everywhere, with the harbour apparently the main focus of attention. My mind went back to a day in September eight years earlier when, once again, I had just arrived in a new country. The place then was Beirut airport, and I had come to take up a fresh post, teaching Arab and Armenian boys in the old city of

Jerusalem in the Hashemite Kingdom of Jordan. As we left the airport we were met by a human flood, clearly in great excitement. It was as if the Kop at Anfield had just let out after a Liverpool victory, only the flowing Arab robes had now replaced the red and white scarves. On that occasion the crowds were returning home from a public execution. At Torshavn the reality was rather less macabre.

My arm was now grabbed by two young men wearing the traditional head-dress of the islanders, who spoke to me in Farocse. I could not understand what they said, but their intentions were quite clear—they wanted me to join them in their boat. By now I had become half-aware of what was afoot, as though the very mien of my abductors had communicated this intuition to me. With a heavy rucksack on my back and still clutching my precious rods, I followed them down the vertical quay-ladder, the lower rungs of which trailed treacherous sea-wrack, and into their open boat. Soon they were pulling for the open sea.

It so happened that my arrival had exactly coincided with the start of a Grindadrap, the Faroese whale-hunt. I had come to fish the sea-trout, now it was to be the whales. The scenes I witnessed around me appeared to be all confusion, though I discovered later that the sequence of events was strictly regulated and deep-rooted in the island's long traditions. Someone, somewhere above the town, had been gazing out to sea, perhaps watching the Copenhagen boat come in, when he had spotted the plumes of spray which betray the presence of a school of whales. He in turn had uttered the cry of 'Grindabod' (the whale) which was taken up by others until the whole township was involved, just as the shout of 'thar she blows', given by lookouts on the old-time whalers, had brought all hands to action stations. The speed with which the excitement spread was like a spark of fire that falls upon the stubble where, animated by the breeze, it kindles into flame, whose tongues then leap from blade to blade until the whole meadow is ablaze in a dancing conflagration.

It may happen in any part of the Faroes at any time. In fact it was to be the first and only sighting of this particular year. The response to the cry is both dramatic and immediate. The shops empty and close their doors, banks shut, schools let out their pupils and all work and business ceases. The young and able-bodied men in the district run for their whaling spears and head down to the boats, whilst the women and children come out to watch or to make ready on the shore—it would have brought bad luck to take a woman in the boats. Others had even climbed the rooftops for a grandstand view. The old men too come down to stare, and perhaps relive in their memories the epic battles of other years. I was told that even surgeons, in the midst of operations, have laid aside their scalpels in favour of the whaling knives! Churches, likewise, lose their congregations should the whales be sighted on a Sunday.

In years gone by the Grindadrap also took place in the Isles of Shetland, Orkney and the Hebrides, though never with quite the same fervour as in the Faroes. I heard a story in the Shetlands that, when the whales chose to enter the voes on the Sabbath Day, even the Sabbath was not respected. In fact the minister at Dunrossness had been in the middle of his sermon one Sunday afternoon when the cry had gone up. Hastily he brought his discourse to an end with the words 'I have only one final word to say, my brethren, that is, let us all have a fair start, just a fair start'.

As in Britain, the sporting parson is no rarity in the Faroes and some have even been elected 'Grindaformadur' or whaling captain. He is the one who will control the operation once the boats put out to sea. In this respect he is like a combined fleet admiral and master of foxhounds. For the purposes of whaling, the islands are split into four districts and each will hold elections to choose its Grindaformadur.

The history of the Grindadrap is a long one and in the course of time has gathered round it many superstitions. For instance, it is most unlucky for the boat containing the parson to get between the whales and the shore. It is also unlucky to have a woman with an unborn child present at the slaughter. Sometimes the boats encounter great difficulty in driving the whales shorewards, but this can be put right if the church doors are left open. I read of one old custom that had long since died out and I quote from an old paper.

> No boat leaves the place without striking up a song of praise to the Lord as a thanksgiving for the gift. It is a solemn sight to behold the boats as they, often in the quiet midnight hour of the clear nights, glide over the glassy level of the sea, and hear the note of praise sounding over the calm ocean.

Our little boat carried five, two were at the oars, with myself in the stern and another two in the bows who would do the driving. As we cleared the harbour entrance, I saw the surface of the sea covered with an armada of small craft. There must have been two hundred of them and, though most were under oars, a few had outboards. The one that carried the Grindaformadur flew its little pennant from the mast and all eyes were on it for signals. Two things are needed for a successful drive, a flooding tide and a good beach on which to ground the quarry. Both were in our favour, with the deep water of Torshavn harbour yielding to provide a gently-sloping, sandy strand at its head.

The location of the whales presented no problem as the fountains of spray could now be seen clearly. The whole flotilla manoeuvred to outflank them and great care was taken not to alarm the school. Once we had gained the advantage of the seaward side, the driving could begin. This was accomplished by splashing rocks into the sea a few yards behind them, and for this purpose we carried two hefty stones in our bows, each painted white and secured to a rope, the other end of which was made fast round one of the thwarts. The lads in the bows stood, throwing out the stones, retrieving and throwing out again. This splashing apart, the boats were almost silent. Whispered conversation, the chug chug of a few outboards, the creaking of oars on the thole-pins, the play of water against timber, these now were the only sounds. In a school of whales about one fifth will surface to blow at any one time, and on this reckoning we had upwards of a hundred whales beneath us. All seemed to be going well until the whole school dived, changed course and, passing under our boats, showed again to the east.

At a signal from the Grindaformadur the whole operation was repeated with the boats rowing once more to gain the seaward positions. As a naval evolution, it was near perfect, the rag-tag and bobtail fleet working with that strong and ancient discipline of all hunting folk. Nearly two hours had passed since the armada first sailed, and now the leading boats were passing the breakwater with the whales heading for the fateful ground. At this point I came ashore and began to make my way down the thronged quayside.

Other boats as well pulled into the side, and I could see that those which were left were occupied by all the young bloods. Once the leading whales were some thirty yards from the shoreline they were deliberately stampeded by a cacophony of banging, shouts and fiendish cries and many on the quay took up the din. The foremost whales surged ahead in their panic, setting up a tidal wave which, as it receded, left them stranded high and dry. These were quickly despatched by skilled butchers, who were already in position, and, with the help of grapnels, hauled up clear of the water. Behind them the scene was frenzied chaos. Some men stood in the boats and thrust their spears into the whales and many followed their spears into the sea. Others completely lost their footing and also joined the whales which, in their turn, were thrashing wildly, their massive tails seeming to dwarf the boats and several were overturned. Some men were even trying to ride the whales into the shore. The waters rapidly began to turn to crimson, and I saw with my eyes what Macbeth had seen only in his visions of the night, 'the multitudinous seas incarnadine'. Meanwhile ashore, the gangs were working furiously, as whale after whale was slaughtered and hauled to dry land.

72

Remembering that I still had to find a bed for the night, I left the quay and made my way into the town, already feeling pangs of sympathy for these gentle and harmless creatures I had helped to chase. They were not fish, but warm-blooded mammals with temperaments and sympathies akin to our own—perhaps in the long chain of evolution—even our ancestors. It was their simplicity that was their undoing for, being herd animals, they must stick together and keep with the pack, come what may. The subsequent waves of whales, which followed the leaders to their own destruction, need not have done so. Having got the message ahead of them, they should have turned around and gained the freedom of the oceans once again. They did not do so because it was not in their nature to reason; the herd instinct was what predominated and thus ensured their fate.

The whales in question were the North Atlantic pilot whales and the largest bulls would have measured around 36 feet. For more than four hundred years the Grindadrap has been an integral part of the overall economy of the islands, an economy chiefly linked to the seas. Nothing is wasted following a hunt and, once the volume of a catch has been assessed, the carcases are cut up and meat distributed to every household in the particular whaling district, no special privilege being given to those who had made the kill possible. The old and infirm, the women and children, all would get their shares to be salted away against the winter months ahead.

When I arrived in the Torshavn hotel for my first night in this new land my heart was heavy with a natural sadness, although I knew that a stranger's sympathy did nothing to put food into mouths that were hungry. Since that time the conservation lobby has vastly increased in size and grown worldwide, and the Faroese themselves, although not abandoning their centuries-old hunt, have nevertheless made concessions to it. The harpoons and whaling spears are now banned and only sufficient whales are culled for food purposes, with subsequent schools left unmolested. But do they need to continue it at all? My guess is that it is probably less necessary today than it was in times past, but something that is so bound up with tradition and with a people's history, culture and lore is not yielded lightly, even though the Faroese appreciate the need to conserve.

My abduction from the quay that evening had at least taught me one thing—a sure and certain cure for seasickness following a long and rough sea passage. I also wondered how many others had gone whaling carrying only a two-piece flyrod in their hand! The Grindadrap, however, was to have one lasting and damaging effect upon my subsequent sea-trout fishing in the islands, which I was soon to discover.

I had planned fourteen days fishing here and would then take ship from Torshavn to Lerwick for five more days with my old friends at the Bridge of Walls in Shetland for a final shot on the voes, which had teased me so much the previous season. By then it would be time to fly back to Merseyside to get the boys' club under way for September.

The fishings on Faroes are nothing if not extensive and mainly confined to the five largest islands of Streymoy, Eysturoy, Sandoy, Vagar and Sudoroy, which have some forty lakes between them as well as numerous places where salmon and sea-trout can be fished for in the fiords and river mouths. Faced with so much water, I had to be selective and decided to divide my time between two bases, spending eight days at Saksun on Streymoy, where I had arranged to stay at the home of Mr and Mrs Ole Jacob Magnussen, and the remaining six on the island of Sandoy, where I would take potluck over finding accommodation; both would put me close to excellent sea-trout lakes.

A bus from Torshavn brought me to Saksun, the route winding its way northwards along the length of the island and passing several small settlements with neat, trim houses, mostly of timber and painted in gay colours, outside many of which lines of fish were drying in the sun. Each twist and turn of the road opened up new expanses of sea with the dark contours of further islands out beyond. Inland, the valley floors were without trees, but fresh and inviting like newly-brushed billiard cloths in varying shades of green, which gradually yielded to the browns and sombre greys of rock that rose steeply above them, where shadows of cloud played and sea birds wheeled in endless skies.

The Magnussens were there to greet me when I arrived at Saksun, and seldom have I stayed with more delightful people. Their timber house was large and comfortable and I was fed like a fighting-cock. Both spoke perfect English and from them I learnt much of life on the islands. Ole Jacob was like many another in the Faroes, part farmer and part fisherman. Possessing his own boat, he longlined in the bay for cod, saithe and haddock. He told me of one occasion when, as a boy, he was out with his father, and each time they were about to lift a fish into the boat a shark appeared from nowhere to strip it from them. Intending to get rid of him, the young Magnussen plunged his sheath-knife deep into the shark's back. The following day, as they were hauling again on the same ground, the shark returned to repeat his tricks, whereupon he reached over and reclaimed his knife.

Perhaps because they were fishermen, they both had an instinctive understanding of a fellow fisherman, readily appreciating his peculiar whims and odd hours; and I was to keep unusual hours during my time there. From the start, I felt very much at home in Saksun.

If my lodgings were superb, their setting was such as to make me feel that I was living on the very brim of the world itself; a green valley bottom, flanked on either side by almost sheer rock, from whose summit white tongues of water reached to lick the sea. By the shore, a little cluster of houses, not regimented in terraces but haphazard and bright, as if they had grown there of their own accord like the meadow flowers around them. Across the valley a white-washed Lutheran church beneath the mountain. Just before the land fell away to the sea, the Magnussen's house stood in splendid isolation, proud as a last sentinel. Further still, and the long arms of rock which embraced the valley almost clasped each other, allowing a narrow inlet for the sea, and thus providing a sheltered anchorage from the boundless ocean which lay beyond.

Following my long journeyings and with my base firmly established, I was by now itching to feel the rod in my hands again and the green turf beneath my feet, and that afternoon I set out to find the lake. The weather, however, had turned decidedly unpleasant and a cold rain was beginning to drive in off the sea. The accompanying mists obscured the views, but I managed to find the water.

On this first afternoon I was very much feeling my way and decided to put up a Black Pennel on the bob, an Alexandra in the middle and a Bloody Butcher on the tail. The first is a very useful allrounder and serves well anywhere, a thoroughly good insurance fly: the other two are outright flashers, but both had worked well in the Shetland voes so they could do the same here. I was soon starting to catch brownies, but all of them little fellows, returned to the water. It always amazes me that such small fish will take these large and gaudy flies so freely. I was fishing size eights and it was not unusual to catch one that was scarcely bigger than the fly itself. These stunted brownies, which share the sea-trout waters, belong to the third world, over-populated and seldom free from hunger. How different their lives must be from the real sheiks of the trout tribe, the ones who inhabit green palaces of weed on the mosaic floors of the chalkstreams, and can afford to laze away their time, ignoring the myriad of flies that sail across their domes.

The weather was worsening fast as the rains drove harder on a north wind, cold enough to numb my fingers. The barometer must have been plummeting, and conditions were far from what one would choose for catching sea-trout. I had, however, travelled a long way for this and there was nothing for it but 'to hack it', as the marines would say, even though the damp was beginning to get to my spirit. It was then that I had a take from something more like what I was looking for, and after a strenuous contest I netted a fine sea-trout of 3 pounds to the Bloody

Butcher. Perseverance was rewarded, and my first Faroese sea-trout came against all the odds; a fisherman is sustained in the knowledge that the unexpected is only a few casts away. Let him believe this and he will endure almost anything.

It was some time before I hit another fish and when it did come it turned out to be a brown trout of a pound and a quarter, which, together with one more sea-trout of the same size brought my first afternoon to an end. A brief diary entry reminds me painfully that I packed in because my fingers had become too cold to fish any more. My hosts were delighted that I brought fish home and gave me high marks for sticking it out.

That evening, Mrs Magnussen spread before me the first of her splendid meals, consisting of a whole roast fowl served with a red jelly, which tasted like crab apple. The bird was in fact a puffin and both this and the guillemot I was later to be given tasted quite delicious. Not surprisingly, the harvest of seabirds and their eggs, like the harvest of the whales, is an important food source throughout the islands. As on Foula their capture from the cliff ledges is a perilous occupation, but here the puffin is also caught ashore, where it is taken on the wing by means of an elongated net, similar to a lacrosse net. This is a sport for true athletes, calling for steady nerves, a quick eye, agility and an all-out effort. For my breakfasts I ate these eggs from the cliffs, which I expected would taste fishy, but they were not that way at all. Had it not been for their shape, and the colour of their shells, I would have thought them hens' eggs; they were surely the most free of all free-range ones.

Part of Faroese lore has it that the weather always takes a turn for the worse following a Grindadrap; this year proved to be no exception. The curse of the whales was well and truly on my head now and was to pursue me relentlessly. The rains and chilling winds persisted and I only enjoyed one day of decent weather at Saksun when it was pleasant to be out fishing.

Because of the northern latitude, the winters, though mild, are long and dark, but at mid-summer the sun sets for less than five hours, giving twilight all night long. I took advantage of this fact and on several mornings rose at 3.00 am to go to the lake. There was no need to disturb my hosts, as breakfast was already set and my faithful alarm-clock would do the rest. I had always known that the dawn of the day was a good time to fish as well as being a golden time just to be abroad. Fishermen who love the evening rise are familiar enough with the sun's setting, but its particular beauty is, for me at least, forever tinged with sadness, since it bears with it the shades of our mortality. At the birth of a new day, however, whenever I have been in time to greet the dawn, I have felt the springs of youth renewed; light's triumph over darkness lies at the heart of all creation. We miss so much for no better reason than we lie too long in bed.

By 3.30 am I was on my way. No one else was astir in the valley at this hour, but I was never on my own during these early morning treks. Always a friendly oyster-catcher marched beside me and even waited at the door for me to emerge. With his long orange bill and bright red legs he kept pace, sometimes running, sometimes in short bursts of flight and piping all the way. Maybe he was happy because at last he had found a human being who knew the proper time to rise, or perhaps he was bestowing a special Faroese blessing upon me. In an epic poem of the islands the hero, who rescues the people from Danish tyranny, is cast in the mould of an oyster-catcher. The Faroese are not a sentimental breed, but they do have a soft spot for this 'little bird by the shore'. In their language he is 'Tjaldur' and has become their national emblem. As Tjaldur and I walked alone at the break of each new day down this valley of the gods, I felt a strange new freedom, as though I was the first, or perhaps the last, man on the earth.

I began to fish soon after 4.00 am. If the hour was golden the weather certainly was not. By the time I got back home at 11.30 am in heavier rain still, I had killed three sea-trout weighing five and a quarter pounds. All the flies had scored this time, the Connemara Black having now replaced the Black Pennell. Four more fish were lost and I had learnt another lesson. The cause of the losses was a dropper pulling out, and another fine fish had gone the same way the day before. Up to this point I had been using readymade nine foot casts with two droppers, manufactured by a well-known tackle firm. I resolved there and then never to use tailor-made casts again, and I never have. Back at the lake that evening I rose four more and lost another. There was no doubt that the lake was full of sea-trout.

By now I had only three days left at Saksun, and wondered how much longer the curse of the whales was going to last, but not even my perseverance could win me any respite, and the north wind turned to a full-strength gale. In a valley, enclosed as we were by deep walls of rock, it played every trick it knew and appeared to come from all directions at the same time. My line, when I could get it out, was blown clean off the water on several occasions, and I was forced to call it a day.

The following morning, my diary records that conditions were good, save for a very high water level in the lake. I made the early start again and even my little black and white companion seemed to have found a new optimism—could Tjaldur annul the ocean's curse? By midday I had creeled four sea-trout, moved another and played and lost a salmon.

As I lay in bed that night, tucked up warm in my downy quilt, I dreamt that my final day would be a real bonanza one. Whales or no whales the sun had shown itself at last, and surely he had the power to break the spell that had dogged my footsteps up till now? Alas, it was not to be. When I peered through my window at 3.00 am that morning, the weather was as fierce as ever and I decided to curl up and go back to sleep. I did manage to make a start at 9.00 am and fished till 4.00 pm, bringing home one sea-trout of a pound and a half, the only fish to move all day. My final tally at Saksun was sixteen fish, weighing twenty nine pounds, but I knew that I had only scratched the surface.

My heart was heavy as I left the place and said goodbye to my hosts, who had looked after me so well and taken me into their home, as if I had been a son. At Torshavn I boarded a trawler and was soon pitching through choppy seas to the island of Sandoy: most of my fellow passengers were some very sturdy-looking sheep, not the most communicative of travellers, but they did prepare me for what was to come. I found accommodation alright, but no one who could speak any English. Our troops had occupied these islands in the war, for they were in a very strategic position, and many of the islanders had learnt English during this time, but, as the years had passed, this facility had largely disappeared. Against all reason we British seem to imagine that all foreigners should be able to speak our tongue and feel very frustrated when they cannot. It is partly a legacy from the days of Empire and partly a cover for our unwillingness to learn other languages. Signs and gestures may communicate basic needs, but they are hardly adequate for building up relationships. I was in two minds whether or not to return to Saksun, but I had come to fish Sandsvatn lake and so decided to put up with a period of living like a Trappist monk.

Sandsvatn was a splendid-looking water, more extensive than the one at Saksun, and lying in a long flat valley. The weather too showed signs again that it was starting to pick up, but the effort to sustain it proved too much. Due to the rains, the lake was now over its banks and its waters heavy and coloured. In fact, I only got onto it twice, when I managed to catch two more sea-trout and turn another two, but they were four more than I could reasonably have expected. Instead, I visited two smaller lakes there, Storavatn and Littlavatn, where I enjoyed good sport with half-pound brownies.

I had experienced sadness over the slaughter of the whales at Torshavn but no feelings of guilt—after all, I had been hijacked onto the hunt—even so, the whole archipelago had suffered under their curse and none had been exempt. My brief stay, however, if not producing heavy bags, had convinced me of the huge potential of these remote fishings, and I had the waters completely to myself.

The scene has changed in more recent times. The Faroese have come to enjoy a growing prosperity—their own airport on the island of Vagar, regular car ferries plying between the islands, new hotels everywhere and fish-farming on a large scale, including salmon rearing on many of the fiords—so this, in turn, has produced more leisure and resulted in greater pressure on the fishings. Licences and permits are now required.

That the fishing would grow in popularity and become more regulated was, perhaps, to be expected, but a recent letter from a friend in Torshavn has informed me of other problems now affecting the fisheries, and amongst them he mentions pollution and the impact that new-built power stations have had on certain lakes and rivers. Sea-trout, in particular, have decreased in numbers and salmon and sea-trout stocks are now supplemented by the introduction of fry from the hatcheries. Throughout my fishing career I have observed the slow and inexorable decline of so many of our own home waters, and this has made me cherish all the more the memory of my visit to these lonely isles with their unsullied waters of almost virginal purity. The letter made me sad because I imagined that Faroes, at least, would be inviolable. It seems now that unless we come to our senses and change our ways, the wild creatures with which we share this planet will soon find there is no sanctuary anywhere.

I am assured, however, that there is still some very good fishing to be found in the Faroes and the fisherman from overseas is always a welcome visitor. My only advice to others who may go to sample it for themselves would be to steer clear of the Grindadrap, whatever else they do!

Chapter 6

Siren Voices on a Western Wind

W hen my ship—the SS *Tjaldur* no less—had steamed out of Torshavn, bound for Lerwick, I stayed on deck to watch the islands darken and fade beyond the phosphorescent glow of her furrowed wake and, as the last pinnacle of rock finally dipped beyond the grey rim of the sea, I promised myself that I would return to fish the Faroes' shores again in kinder weather. More than twenty-five Augusts have come and gone since then and still my pledge is unfulfilled, and the reason for this was that I heard the siren voices of another isle and fell bound under the spell, which ever since has drawn me, like a magnet, for more than a quarter of a century.

I have never fished in Norway nor in Iceland, in Canada nor New Zealand: I have not cast for giant perch in the waters of the Nile nor for the fighting mahseer of the Indian subcontinent; and I have never wet my line on any of the charming little rivers of Europe. The world is full of beautiful places and man's allotted span is all too brief. Enough for me now to know that the pleasantest place in all the world to fish is Ireland, and that is not so much a fact as the opinion of one who, having heard the music, was destined to become a self-confessed Hibernophile. The fatal attraction that the Emerald Isle has for me, as a fisherman, is beyond analysis, perhaps because it is something that is felt in the deep places of the heart and the gut, rather than anything rational that the mind can grasp. A young man falls in love—he knows not how nor why for the whole affair is too elusive ever to be caught in a net of words. We may, however, disentangle certain threads that form at least a part of the web of Ireland's unique quality as the great enchantress.

My geography lessons at school taught me that Ireland is shaped like a saucer with the rim of its coastline rising from the oceans to provide splendid mountains, which fall away to yield the broad interior plain, and this has produced a land of waters; the eye can never wander far without picking up its bright reflections. The mountains catch the clouds which sweep in with the Atlantic swell, forcing them to drop their rains which, in turn, feed the rivers—mighty rivers like the stately Shannon and a thousand and more lesser ones, some of which drain their Guinness waters off the boglands, leaping and bounding back to the seas on rock-strewn beds beneath spongy banks of heather, whilst others glide more softly, meandering with a pastoral leisure over beds of limestone, where they caress the swaying fronds of water-weed. Many such rivers course in and out of lakes that may be huge expanses that go on and on like inland seas, or little loughs that nestle secretly within the tucks and foldings of the hills.

One cannot drive for long in Ireland without coming to a bridge. And I am an inveterate 'bridge-stopper'. In this wide land there is no urgency, time loses its press and there is little need to hurry. This allows me to indulge my weakness, to pull up, leave the car and lean over the parapet to gaze into the waters there below me. All the streams and rivers of the west hold trout and very many have a run of salmon and sea-trout, or 'white-trout' I should call them, for this is the name the Irish give to their migratory trout. The temptation to set up the rod and cast for the fellow I see rising can be hard to resist, but probably no matter anyway, as most of these waters will be free.

If Ireland is a place of many waters it is also a land of surpassing beauty and never more so than down the western side, where the Atlantic rolls in past small islands, the final footholds of Europe, before sweeping into a fretted coastline, which rises to peaks of mountains, as blue as the grapes' bloom when the sun is on them. The hinterland has been shaped partly by nature and partly by centuries of heroic toil for, though the seas are highly productive, the rockbound earth is unrewarding and the soil remains poor, even with its mulch of wrack. Yet everywhere tiny fields cluster around neat, trim homesteads that crouch low to the land, each bright with its own colourwash that sets off the dark amber of the store of peats, drying in the wind against the winter months. The stones too have their uses for, piled into walls, they separate the fields, some scarce bigger than carpets, but every inch won from the unyielding granite with a patient toil.

In summertime the hedgerows glow with fuchsia beneath whose trailing bells of fire clumps of montbretia shyly raise their flaxen heads. Heather and honeysuckle, mountain ash, furze and cotton-grass add their lustre to the scene. The light in this westland has a character all its own, a soft ethereal quality that gives emphasis to the many shades of colour, all of which exist only in a state of perpetual change, as fleeting clouds play across the face of the sun, interspersing their shadows.

Small wonder then that artists are always painting these wild landscapes, and galleries and picture shops across the country are full of their works. I have searched long and hard to buy a canvas that I can look at for eleven months each year and, as I do so, feel again the yielding turf beneath my feet, smell the faint, sweet scent of bog-myrtle and catch the deep guttural cry of red-throated divers as they pass high above me. I have not bought yet, not because the Irish artists are not excellent, but simply because these landscapes refuse to be caught and held: in the tremble of the light they are forever in transition, never staying still. A painter may paint the dancer but he can never paint the dance.

Perhaps the brightest thread of all in the tapestry of Ireland's magic is the people themselves, and in this respect the man who comes to fish has one clear advantage over the casual visitor. The tourist comes to see as much of the country as he can in the short space that his holiday affords. He is always on the move, writing up his diary in the evenings, then spreading out his maps and already his mind is on tomorrow's route. He will, of course, be charmed by the Irish he meets on the way, their courtesy, easy manners and their humour, but he can never really get to know them.

The fisherman, on the other hand, stays in one place and frequently returns there time and time again. His chosen sport in any case makes him a member of a great freemasonry, and by the sea or lough and beside the rivers he will meet many another.

Ireland is a land of great sportsmen, whether it be the breeding of fine horses or dogs, the wild sports of the countryside or, as some would have it, the even wilder national sports of hurley and Gaelic football, and readily takes another sportsman to her heart. Few cottages in the west will be without a fishing-rod of sorts, tucked away in a special corner or mounted and ready for action, as it lies on pegs in the wall of the byre.

Ireland has been home and nursery to saints and scholars, warriors and men of letters, and traces of all four are to be found in the Irish character still, but the one thing in which they all excel is the art of conversation, and how it flows. Time here is never at a premium and the day is given for talk. I pull the boat into the shore where a fellow is making a 'dint of hay', as he says, 'for there's a brave drying on the wind', and he comes down to ask if 'Yourself is after taking any fish'. It is pleasant to leave the boat, rest the arms, and stretch the legs, but even more so to listen to the lilt of the soft brogue with many a well-turned phrase and a choice of words which, if not grammatical, is nonetheless pure poetry. I inquire about a tiny lough that links above to the one I am on, and ask if the white-trout find their way to it. He does not believe they do for 'the heron comes not at it'. A small cloud appears and sits, like a cap, on the blue crest of the mountain in front of us, and we wonder if it's going to rain.

He's 'afeard for the hay' and it isn't even his—he is only doing it to help out the old man. We English are far too niggardly in the use of words, trading them with a care and measured discretion, as if afraid they may betray too many hidden defences, and, though wine may bring a measure of release to the Englishman's tongue, he prefers to keep it firmly on the leash. The Irish have no such inhibitions and, whether they are singing the sad old ballads or merely passing the time of day, their words issue with a spontaneity, like a lark springing from a meadow to trill his sweet song in the summer's air.

The burden of Ireland's history—the weight of the wrongs that have been done there—bears heavy on her shoulders, and a wrong has never died in Ireland. Such is the perspective of history that the evils of Strongbow, Cromwell and the Black and Tans are all only as yesterday. Just as the sky is tinged with crimson rays by a sun that has already set, so too is the Ireland that I love, a land of so much beauty, gaiety and humour, tinged by a lasting sorrow emanating from her past. Those who read her history and literature, listen to her ballad songs, and travel her western seaboard will hear for themselves this melancholy beat within her ancient heart.

There are, of course, many other places where the waters and landscape are superb and the people open and welcoming and I have been to some of them. Yet Ireland remains on her own. It is as though geography and climate, history and accident have all combined in some mysterious alchemy to make the perfect place in which to go fishing. And the weather can be just as bad here as anywhere else. The difference is that it seems to matter so much less. Gentle showers arch the valleys with their rainbows and the land is often wrapped in mist. Some forty inches of rain fall each year, but every inch of that is only an inch of Irish rain. When the mist starts to trickle in little droplets down your neck, then is the moment you are likely to be hailed with 'A fine soft day, thank God'.

The first visit I ever made to Ireland was a fleeting one and carried out under very different circumstances just after the war. I was serving at that time as a lieutenant, Royal Marines, aboard an aircraft carrier. One Friday evening we had anchored in Belfast Lough. The subaltern of marines, usually known on board as 'Soldier', does not keep watch at sea, but he does take his turn of watchkeeping when in harbour. That first night I had the Middle Watch. Four bells into the watch—2.00 am to the landlubber—I was growing aware that the wind had freshened to the point where it was gusting to near gale force. I made my way up to the bridge and began to take compass bearings on the shore and these led me to suspect that we might be dragging anchor. The call of duty was clear (though not inviting) and there was nothing for it but to make my way aft and shake the captain. With the natural caution of a junior officer, and feeling something of the trepidation of those early Christians at the brink of the Colliseum, I entered his cabin and immediately passed under the steely eye of Southey's famous portrait of Nelson, and I could swear I heard England's greatest sea captain say, 'Go on, Soldier, shake the old man'. As things turned out the captain was grateful for the intervention and before long I heard the engines getting underway.

The following day I was to play cricket for the ship against the naval station in Derry and the bus ride provided me with my first glimpse of the Irish countryside and pretty sombre it was. The forty inches of rain seemed determined to fall all at once, obliterating the Sperrin Mountains. Even Derry's proud walls were weeping and, of course, no ball ever left the bowler's hand.

Fourteen years after this I made my first visit as a fisherman, coming to Oughterard in Co Galway. Now a parson, and still an impoverished Boys' Club Leader, I travelled by scooter. My trusty Lambretta was festooned like a Christmas tree, with full panniers on either side, and suitcase and fishing bag tied with string to the rack above the rear mudguard; a bulging rucksack bit into my shoulders and rods and net were slung behind me. From the Army and Navy Stores I had bought an old RAF flying-suit which I had reproofed against the weather. This admirable garment zipped right up the middle and finally disappeared into a pair of Wellington boots. It kept me both warm and dry.

My appearance as a dashing aviator, however, was soon dispelled by the little scooter which never exceeded forty miles per hour. As the sole means of transport for a month's fishing it was very far from ideal. Irish ghillies to a man, preferred to use their bikes rather than hazard themselves on the pillion seat. Nevertheless, it seldom let me down. On the one occasion that I did come off it on a slippery corner outside Dublin it started first kick, and my rods remained intact.

Oughterard lies on the western shore of Lough Corrib. Here I stayed at the Corrib Hotel where I was greeted on my entrance by the sight of a truly massive brown trout. It was a fish of more than twenty pounds weight, which is displayed to this day in the foyer beside the reception desk. Over the years its benign presence on the wall must have done much to boost the bookings in this anglers' hotel.

Corrib is the largest lough in Eire, receiving its intake of water at the top end through an underground channel from Loughs Calla and Mask, and many rivers and streams feed into it. At its southern end it runs out through the famous weir at Galway into the sea at Galway Bay. Throughout its length it is studded with hundreds of islands, fringed by shallows. Ireland has two chains of big limestone lakes which are well known for their large trout. One is set in the central plain, and this contains waters with the highest pH content: these are Loughs Sheelin, Derravarragh, Owel and Ennell. The average size of trout caught is over two pounds, and fish of eight pounds are taken each season on the fly. The lakes of the western chain are larger in size and less alkaline in content: these are Loughs Corrib, Mask, Carra, Conn and Arrow. They too hold splendid trout and fish of four to six pounds are not uncommon at the height of the season. Also present are the big ferox or cannibal trout, whose weight is in double figures and are only caught by deep-trolling. Corrib has its salmon, and pike and perch seem to flourish everywhere.

Lough Corrib is probably best known for its mayfly fishing, which starts around the 20th of May and lasts for about four weeks. The hatch can be profuse. It is about this time that many a businessman, sweating it out in city offices from London to Glasgow, Dublin to Birmingham, begins to get restive and finds his mind not wholly on his work. He is waiting for one thing, that call from the west of Ireland from his boatman to say the hatch has started. Armed with this summons, he can now forget his worries as he heads for the shores of Corrib. Mostly the boats will be dapping the natural fly, known as the greendrake, and bags of up to twenty fish for two rods are often caught. They will be heavy bags, too, for the mayfly, the largest of the family of upwinged flies (the ephemeroptera), brings the big trout up to the surface.

Like other waterborne flies, the mayfly hatches from eggs which lie in the silt of the lake floor; it then becomes a nymph, and almost all of its brief life of one to two years is spent beneath the water. At this stage it is an ugly looking creature, quite lacking in grace, and its days in this watery nursery are dismal, dark and dangerous, for fish feed heavily on nymphs of every kind. If, however, it can survive these perils and reach the surface of the lake in May, then, like Cinderella, it is destined not only to be transformed, but also to attend the ball. Once on the surface, it frees its wings from the nymphal case that has enclosed them and, as soon as they have dried, rises in the sun, now no longer a nymph but a subimago or dun. A few hours later the final transformation occurs, when it changes from the somewhat drab appearance of the dun into the full brilliance of an imago or spinner. In the hymnwriter's words it has 'changed from glory into glory'. Now the summer sky is filled with joy, as it forms the stage for an aerial ballet of sheer perfection, the love-dance of the greendrakes. But Cinderella had to quit her ball by midnight, and already the hours are running out. With mating completed, the female drops once more to the lake to deposit her eggs, which will renew the whole life-cycle. Her midnight hour has struck and there she dies, her veined and gossamer wings spreadeagled on the water's surface. Through all the changing scenes of life (including death)—from nymph to dun to spinner and finally to spent fly—the greendrake is food for trout.

In recent years the mayfly hatches have become a good deal less predictable, for what reason I do not fully know, as they vary from fair to poor.

Newcomer that I was to Oughterard, the mysteries of Corrib were quite unknown to me then. I was thoroughly green and entirely dependent upon, and to some extent at the mercy of, my boatman. The hotel had arranged that a man would meet me at nine o'clock next morning. Mattie Mons arrived, a well-built, red-headed lad of eighteen summers, who farmed some four miles up the lough shore, close to where he kept his boat. He turned out to be a splendid young man, full of enthusiasm, with the strength of an ox and eager only that his man catch fish. But he only knew one way of doing it and that was to troll. This was certainly unusual in an Irish boatman. As a breed they both expect and hope their clients will be fishermen, and this means fly-fishers, but Mattie was not a professional boatman. If farming duties allowed, he filled in only when the hotel was stuck. A keen angler himself, he used to go out on the lough with his mate every Sunday after Mass, where they would troll long lines behind the outboard, chugging at low revs.

I would have much preferred to fly-fish, but quickly made up my mind to go along with Mattie's ideas rather than risk having no boatman at all, and I was happy just to be out on these famed waters. Each morning for the next few days he turned up on his bike, and was the first of several boatmen to spurn my offer of a ride on the pillion seat. He also came with a good supply of small trout, some four to six inches long which he had procured the evening before from the stream. He set up a rod for me, mounted one of these small trout on a spinning-flight and off we set.

August, anyway, can be rather a dour month on these big loughs where the feeding is so plentiful. By now the mayfly will have been long over and for much of July the fish will have been concentrating their attention on the perch fry. Few flies are seen to be hatching on the lake's surface, and the fish seem to succumb to a general lethargy and are probably feeding much deeper. Mattie was confident that the fly would be no good, a view I could not completely share after seeing the nice trout one wet fly-fisherman was bringing back each evening. But Mattie knew what he was up to and was perfectly happy to row me round all day long and it was very pleasant. Two days at least were blazing hot, the kind of days that make fly-fishermen start to troll anyway. An element of the unknown was also present, since a spinning bait could equally well be seized by a salmon, a ferox, a pike or a perch. The red-hot days yielded perch only, but we managed a few trout on the others. They were decent enough fish, far better than I was used to catching at home, but nothing compared to what Corrib can produce. Several fish hit the bait without being hooked, and by the end of the day Matties's supply of small trout was about exhausted. I too began to grow exhausted, not from exertion on my part, but from the sheer tedium of the troll.

One day, however, turned out to be far from dull and might well have been the last day either of us was to fish again. A good breeze was blowing as we started out with large fleecy clouds hiding the sun from time to time—a perfect kind of day for the wet-flies. I suppressed my longing as Mattie, using his engine, headed for a large island. Someone at some time had built a house upon it, now unoccupied. That in itself must have been quite a feat as all materials and labour would have had to have been ferried over. Mattie informed me that one or two lives had been lost in the process, though he thought they had been drunk at the time. We rounded this island and spent the whole day trolling off the leeward shore, blissfully unaware of how the weather had changed. The moment we left the shelter of the island in the evening the prospect looked entirely different: between us and home the lough had become an angry sea with rolling white horses everywhere.

It was by no means obvious that we should set out for home at all and, had the weather been any worse, we would certainly have stayed on the island. We had food in the trout that we had caught and we could have built a large fire, which might have been seen from the mainland and taken as a signal of our intentions. We even had a house. Fortunately the wind was coming straight off-shore, which meant that we would be heading into the sea rather than across it, and that was in our favour. By using the engine and adjusting her speed to ride the swell, we felt confident that we could make it with nothing worse than a good soaking. We stowed our rods and gear, using what shelter the bow end provided, and put on oilskins. Mattie filled the tank with petrol, but would not start the engine until he had first cut loose the little bottle that was tied beneath the bow. He then anointed both the boat and ourselves with a sprinkling of the holy water it contained and replaced the bottle. The boat was sturdy enough, and now with a quiet confidence he tugged the engine into life and set our course for home. The ride was bumpy all right as the bows bucketed against the waves, and the engine raced each time her screws came clear of the water. I did my best to act as ballast, watching each wave and adjusting my position accordingly. We shipped a lot of water, but Mattie had the worst of it as he took each drenching straight between the eyes.

I realised then that, no matter how experienced he is, the angler must always keep a weather-eye open when out on these big waters. Corrib itself contains sixty-eight square miles of water and Conn and Mask are each about nine miles in length. Storms blow up quickly, whipping these waters into seas, and there are many days each season when no boats put out at all. Hardly surprising, then, that so many of them have their little phials of holy water.

It is not often that I make use of the services of a boatman today. My purse, as well as my natural inclinations to manage things myself, both make for independence, but it was not always that way. In the early years of my lough fishing I used to take one with me, for the hotels expected you to do so, and there was much to be said for going out with someone who really knew the lough well.

I certainly needed a boatman on my first visit to fish for white-trout on the waters of Lough Currane in Co Kerry. Although the fishing is free here, to fish its seventeen mile circumference effectively certainly demands a high degree of local knowledge. It must rank high in the topflight of the Republic's white-trout loughs, producing heavier fish on average than those to be found on most other western fisheries, perhaps because the seas around the Blasket Islands provide richer feeding than those around the Arans.

I stayed at the Butler Arms in Waterville, one of three famous Irish hotels, all managed at that time by members of the Huggard family. It was very much a fisherman's hotel, and contained one refinement I have found nowhere else: outside each bedroom door a line-drier was fastened to the wall. Fishermen then were still using the Kingfisher silk lines, and these were always better for being stripped off the reel each evening to dry thoroughly.

At the foot of the very fine staircase was a large area of parquet flooring, always highly polished. In the evening, the day's catch would be laid out there, each group of fish with its own label. Fishermen jealously guard their reputations and become afflicted by a good-natured form of vanity whenever their day has been attended by success, and this gave rise to the pre-dinner ritual —a close inspection of the display on the hall floor. Salmon and white-trout featured predominantly but very occasionally brownies also added their grace to it.

I remember one evening when the floor was more than usually covered with fish. Major-General X had a fine catch of two salmon and six white-trout, Doctor Y had also done well, but pride of place went to a line of plump little brownies, each one a bar of shining gold around the 4-5 ounce mark. These were the bag a thirteen year old had brought back from a mountain stream, and they took my mind back to school holidays of long ago, when I too had cut my teeth on the swift-flowing rivers of Lilliput that ran from the hills. Believe me, monsterhood in trout is not something to be determined in the balances, but something that resides in the mind, and Master Z was as proud and pleased as Punch with his day's treasure.

The hotel had boats on Lough Currane as well as the three smaller loughs, Derriana, Clooaghlin and Namona, connected to it on the northern shore by the Cummeragh River. Tickets were also issued for the Currane River whose final pool—the famous

Butler Pool—is in sight and sound of the Atlantic. I had a week's fishing on these waters and the hotel arranged for Paddy to be my boatman.

I never discovered his second name but he was already into his seventies and, like many of his countrymen, had fought in the trenches of the First World War. He belonged to the great old school of Irish boatmen. I had come to Ireland for a month's fishing, still riding my Lambretta scooter, festooned with panniers, but I warmed quickly to Paddy for, old soldier that he was, he was one of the very few boatmen who ever consented to chance themselves on the pillion of my transport.

Paddy possessed that peculiar gift, which all great boatmen have, of making you fish well. He did this not by imparting instruction—that would be far too presumptuous for, however badly they may be fishing, boatmen hold their clients in great respect. Their skill is much more subtle, and I know that it was from men like Paddy that I came to learn that successful angling is very much a matter of confidence. With many others of his trade he was a man of few words but, when they did come, they were designed to raise the flagging spirit, bring back a sparkle to the cast and the gleam of expectancy to the eye.

'Now, sorr, I am putting you over some of the very best water in all the lough', or maybe, 'I had a gennelman with me last week, sorr, and didn't he raise two grand fish just as we come into this bay?'

Whether or not the statements were true did not matter at all. What mattered was that within the next ten minutes you were stuck into a grand fish yourself. I did not let Paddy down too badly for we brought white-trout home each evening, and good ones too.

In 'King Henry the Fourth' Shakespeare makes Glendower taunt Harry Hotspur with the question 'Know ye not that I can summon spirits from the vasty deep?', and I sometimes wonder whether certain boatmen may not, in fact, possess the same gift. In the Solomon Islands, for instance, the natives know how to call the porpoises.

On our second day out, the weather turned decidedly cold, and poor Paddy started to sneeze and cough a bit. I began to get worried.

'Are you getting a cold, Paddy?', I asked, my chief concern being that I should not lose my man on the sicklist tomorrow. 'Agh, it's only a touch', he replied. 'It's the weather that's in it'.

In my eagerness and simplicity I answered, 'I can put that right, Paddy. You come back to the hotel with me afterwards'.

In the bar that evening Paddy downed a couple of double brandies and was rarin' to go next morning. In fact I thought he was quite recovered, that was until the last drift or two of the day when the old symptoms started to return. The 'medical' side of that week's fishing cost me a small fortune, but Paddy managed to stay the course.

I wanted to have a shot at Butler's Pool and got a ticket to fish

98

it for one hour. The rule was that you had to take a ghillie with you and I soon saw the reason for this. The pool was absolutely bursting with salmon as they lay in layers one above another, and any fool could have hooked one. I asked Paddy what was likely to happen if I did latch onto one of them.

'Well, sorr, the chances are he'll take you straight out to sea. Many's the time I've bin up to me middle in them waves landin' one for a gennelman, so I have'.

I certainly tried hard to catch one legitimately but without success. My flies brushed against their flanks, and I am sure the bigger ones were telling the smaller ones not only the name of the fly but also who had tied it. Perhaps it was just as well. Paddy's cold might easily have turned to pneumonia had I sent him water-skiing into the Atlantic. And how much brandy would that have cost me?

Chapter 7

Mighty Mask

O f the big limestone loughs on the western chain my favourite has to be Lough Mask to the north of Corrib, which is surely one of the world's great trout waters. On its eastern flank stretch the green plains of Mayo, which roll as pleasingly as the soft brogue on the local tongue. Above its western shore the blue Partry Mountains stand guard with the peaks of Joyce's Country showing clearly to the south. It is a vast expanse of water covering some 20,500 acres in all, ten miles long with an average width of around four miles.

It carries many enchanting islands as well as great reefs of rock which, being limestone, are jagged and needle-sharp and some of these reach far into the middle waters of the lough, where one might expect the deepest places to be. Here they lie hidden just beneath the surface and sharp enough to pierce clean through the boat, making Mask no place for a newcomer to go charging about with an outboard engine. There are days when the barometer rides high and the water looks innocuous enough, as it shimmers in a mirror-calm, but the weather can change quickly, as high winds sweep down from the Partry Mountains to transform it into a surging sea. The true Mask fisherman not only knows his lough in great detail, but also holds it always in a deep respect.

It is, however, the presence of these reefs and shallows that makes the fishing, for they provide those superb long drifts over waters, varying in depth from 3-10 feet, where trout to 4 pounds and more come readily to the fly. The deeper waters over the 20-30 foot contours are home to the ferox, and in 1983 one of $17\frac{3}{4}$ pounds was caught on a spoon-bait off Shindilla Island—just one pound short of the record one, which Thomas Malia had caught in 1934. Bill Scorer, my Irish fishing companion over many years, found himself becalmed one blazing day and decided to try his home-made spoon in the deeps off Devenish Island, whilst he reclined to absorb a tan. That spoon is now attached to his ring of car keys, where its inscription proudly records the $10\frac{1}{2}$ pounder that fell to it.

It was Bill's invitation to join him at Ballinrobe for a week's fishing at the end of June that was my first introduction to the joys of Mask. Ballinrobe is a typical Irish country market town of much character and, by virtue of its position, central to the eastern shore with its extensive shallows and rocky outcrops, is the natural centre for the fishing. In earlier years it had been a garrison town and the shells of the old infantry and cavalry barracks still remain.

I had spent that year working in Northern Ireland in the border town of Strabane in County Tyrone. This too had been a smiling little town, but the recent outbreak of 'the troubles' in the country had left much devastation there. The morning after my hotel had been blown up—it was the only hotel left—someone had passed the comment to me, 'Strabane will make a grand carpark one day'. Few people ventured into the town in the evenings, and the local cinema in the main street had run out of business. Using this cinema building, now gutted of its seats, I endeavoured to run a Youth Centre there that would bring young protestants and catholics together in a recreational setting. It was very much an eleventh hour, bridge-building enterprise, but it had the backing of the Community Relations Commission in Belfast. By the time Bill's invitation arrived, I was more than ready to welcome some respite from the strife around me.

Bill was coming from Dublin where he was a partner in a firm of chartered accountants. He had been born and brought up in Appleby, in the old county of Westmorland, but for many years now had made his home in Eire, where he still lives with his Irish wife and two young daughters. He had by this time become something of an expert on the Mask, for at one stage in his career, in a lull between jobs, he had spent a whole summer in Ballinrobe, living the simple, nomad life out of a tent pitched beside her shores and close by where his boat was moored. Up to then he had worked for high-powered companies and was now determined to exorcize once and for all the rat-race from his system, to take fresh bearings for his life's course, and where better for such an exercise than by Mask's murmuring shores? During that summer he fished it hard, becoming sufficiently familiar with it to work for a time as a boatman there. Today he is still a proud card-holder of the Ballinrobe boatmen's union.

The summer suns, the city office and Dublin's thronging pavements had all conspired to make Bill ready for a break too.

I joined him in Dublin and together we drove across Ireland, arriving in time to secure a boat for the week—Bill had his own outboard—and pick up a cylinder of Calor gas before pitching our tent in the soft evening rain by Caher Bay. Our routine was pretty basic and designed to give us maximum fishing time. The morning shave, bacon and egg breakfast, followed by a quick run into town to keep the camp larder stocked. I say 'stocked' because our adversary turned out to be a stray dog, who prowled around our tent like the hosts of Midian, his mission to turn over our bin and to unstock our larder as quickly as he could. He had a great appetite for our steak suppers. With the chores completed, sandwiches made, camp secured and dog seen off, we would spend the day fishing our teams of wet-flies down the long drifts of the lough.

Lunch would be taken on one of the many islands where we brewed the tea and sat amongst the random scatterings of limestone chips, which lay all around us, sharp and deeply-fissured, and in all kinds of grotesque shapes. Cleaned and nicely mounted, some could have passed as works of modern sculpture. Bill, who has never lacked an eye for a quick bargain, set one up in the sand behind the fire and proclaimed it 'The Violin Player', an early piece by Henry Moore, and I could see exactly what he meant. Sometimes other boats would be taking lunch as well, and it was good to compare notes on the morning's sport, and listen to improbable stories. Tea was always brewed in the 'Volcano', an aptly-named contraption that I have only ever found in Ireland. It is made of tin, the top part being filled with water from the lough and the base containing the little stick fire. Even on wet days the water comes quickly to the boil with the help of a little petrol from the outboard; the fresh tea has a tang about it that is

far superior to the stuff from a thermos flask. I am sure the old
Irish tinkers used to make them, and I would dearly love to get
my hands on one. In my mind they are an integral part of a day's
boat-fishing on the lough.

Back at the tent the day's catch would be laid out on
newspapers and Luke Higgins, who kept The House of the Eagle
inn in Ballinrobe, would buy them from us later that evening.
These splendid Mask trout with their bold markings and deep
bodies were always in great demand. From his earlier exploits Bill
had come to know the local boatmen—he was one of their
number—as well as most of the fishing fraternity in the town,
many of whom would gather for the evening jar in Luke's bar;
and it was there that our footsteps would lead us before the day
was out. If, however, it was a warm and balmy evening we might
try our luck first on the little river Robe which ran nearby. It was
then a delightful chalkstream, a place of joy, with many a good
pool and gentle glide under banks, exuberant with the wild
flowers of summer. One would weep to see it today, for giant
earth-removers have scoured out its living soul to leave a muddy
canal in a desolation of debris. So much for land drainage
schemes!

Arriving at the river-bank on our first evening, we both
marked a fine trout, which we estimated to be around the 3 pound
mark, that was rising steadily in the centre of a wide pool, with a
second fish showing just as freely by the near bank. This also was
a fair fish but nothing like the size of the one in the middle. The
smaller fish presented no problems, but his fellow certainly did,
for he was feeding at the far side of an eddy in the current, making
the drag on the fly almost instantaneous, and any drag would
certainly put him down. To cast for the big one would also mean
casting over the near one, and that would put him down as well.
In any case, it seemed that the only way to get the fly over the big
lad would be to employ a version of what the late Oliver Kite, in
his excellent book *Nymph Fishing in Practice*, describes as 'the
backlash cast'. Such a cast aims at a point above the water and is

made with sufficient force to allow the line to straighten and then recoil back to the left, giving a distinct curl to the cast, which, properly accomplished, enables the fly to cover the fish before the line has time to initiate drag. The cast was going to call for great deftness, and the situation posed one of those nice problems that is the essence of the river dry-fly art.

We decided to try for the easier fish first, hoping to land him without alarming the one in the middle. Bill put up a small, winged Olive and he came at the first attempt, but there was no way he was going to be hauled. He played hard, running line all through the pool, as befitted a lusty trout of a pound and a quarter, whose supper had been so rudely interrupted. Once he was safely in the bag we looked again, but the other one had stopped rising. It was my turn now and, thinking that he would soon settle, I sat amongst the buttercups to smoke my pipe, but he did not resume feeding. On two further evenings we went down to look for him but never saw him again. Clearly we were not the only ones who shared the secret of this pool, and even the corncrakes in the meadow seemed to be laughing at us.

By the time we arrived at Luke's pub, it was as busy and full as ever. Luke was a fine looking man of a somewhat military appearance and both he and his wife, Eileen, were excellent hosts. The bar they kept was full of character too, always dimly-lit with ancient firearms glinting from the walls, for Luke was a keen collector of curios. It was a place of warmth and friendliness where conversation was what mattered—no nonsense here of fruit-machines or piped music. Luke was also a keen fisherman—he could hardly have been otherwise—with a special fondness for Lough Carra, a much smaller lough half a mile to the north-east of Mask.

I have heard Carra described as the most alkaline lake in Europe and I can well believe it. Its water is exceedingly clear, which is often disconcerting when you are fishing, as you tend to see the fish before they take the fly. The lough floor is a white sand and the rocks in the water are covered by a thick deposit of a soft, spongy marl, as if nature had fitted them with fenders. If you happen to hit a rock on Lough Mask it will possibly pierce the boat, but on Carra it is the rock that will be dented. The overall colour of the water is a yellowy green, like weak lime-juice, with the shades varying according to the depth, and much of the shore-line is fringed with large beds of reed. On the western shore, interred in a simple tomb, lie the ashes of George Moore, the celebrated Irish poet who died in England in 1933, whilst, on the hillside behind, stands the burnt-out shell of Moore Hall, the family home, a monument to long-gone and extravagant days.

Whether dapping or casting, Lough Carra is a fascinating place to fish. It certainly holds some very big trout—the average caught will be heavier than that from Mask—and fish of six to seven pounds are caught on the Spent Gnat during the very early mayfly hatch. They are extraordinary trout to look at, some I have caught have been almost pure white in colour, for all trout tend to take their complexion from the environment in which they live. Luke has now retired in Ballinrobe, having sold the pub, and I hope he long continues to sally forth on his beloved waters of Lough Carra.

The hatch of sedges after dark on the big limestone loughs of Ireland can be prolific, but you have to get it right—that is be at the right place at the right time, on the right evening—and you need nerves of steel. These sedges are either the peters or the great red sedge, which is known in Ireland as the murrough. They hatch in the deep water after dark and, once they have emerged from the surface film, begin to scutter their way towards the shore. The flies to use will be the Green Peter or Dark Peter, and the Murrough or Claret Murrough. There is no question, but that these sedges are sufficiently large and succulent to bring the really big trout on the feed, such trout as would never bother to come to the fly at any other times. Many an Irish fly-fisherman has this night-time hatch to thank for his largest ever trout. Niall Fallon in his comprehensive book *Fly-Fishing for Irish Trout* tells most vividly the story of his own record fish, a brown trout of six and a half pounds, which came to a Green Peter on a midland lough, and how, for some time, it actually towed the boat along—the point of his cast was a mere 3 pounds breaking strain—whilst his unhappy companion sat and wrestled in the darkness with a tangle.

There were other evenings when Bill and I went straight to the pub after supper, before setting out once more on Mask to fish the sedge. After the day-time fishing it was somewhat eerie to be creeping under silent oars into Ballinachalla Bay by the light of the stars, and almost frightening to hear the massive trout erupting as they came for these sedges—some of them would have been fish in the five or six pound class. We both tied on Green Peters and fished them dry, even though it was no longer possible to see them on the water. Sometimes we drew the fly across the top, in imitation of the living creature, as it jerked its way in stages across the surface. When it is too dark to see the fly, I suppose one ought to strike each time a fish rises in the area where one thinks one's fly to be, and, failing to do this, I probably missed the one chance I had, but, exciting as it was, we were not successful and returned fishless to our tent.

Irish fishermen on these big loughs are a thoroughly conservative breed, who rely almost wholly on fishing down the drifts with a team of three wet-flies, or else dapping with the live insect, whilst a smaller number seem content with the tedious employment of trolling. They are reluctant to experiment, try a variation of tactics or do anything that diverges from this norm, even on those occasions when the well-tried methods fail to bring results. The dry-fly, for instance, is virtually ignored. There is, however, some justification for this, because, as a general rule, the dry-fly is always likely to be more effective on the smaller loughs. On the huge expanses, such as Mask affords, what hatches of fly there may be will be very localised affairs, and, provided there is a wave on the water, fish which may be rising, will come to the wet-flies just as well.

There remain, however, certain types of conditions—calm, bright days, when small dry-flies do provide for better—and sometimes the only—opportunities for fish. Bill and I discovered this on just such a day one late August when the surface of the lough reflected like a mirror. As we motored up to Lively Bay we could spot occasional rises here and there, but they were few and far between and suggested cruising fish. We had decided to try the very small flies off a rocky shoreline, where we had some help from the sporadic appearances of the faintest of breezes which, when it was there, was just enough to put a little pin-ripple on the water. Within the hour, we each had a trout of over two pounds—Bill's to a size 16 Ant and mine to an equally small Ginger Quill. On days like these, most boats remain tied up and the few that are out will be trolling, but we met up with one, which contained two of Mask's specialists, who had been persevering with traditional wet-flies, if not with much hope, and they were amazed that such tiny flies had worked.

The boatmen, who earn their living on the big loughs, are all fishermen themselves, and hope that their clients will be the same: wet-fly or dappers, for then their days are full of interest and variety. On many occasions, however, their clients turn out to be those who merely want to troll all day, which makes extra work and tedious hours for the boatmen, who begin to long for the 6 pm deadline. It is a strange fact that most experienced boatmen seem able to spot what kind of men their clients are just by watching them approach the boat. Jonjo Malone of Ballinrobe, for example, one of Mask's fine boatmen, reckons to pick up the build of a trolling man from a range of 400 yards. It has been said that the faces of dog-owners betray the breeds of dog that they possess, and, in the same kind of way, the differing gaits of lough-fishers give away their styles of fishing.

When the Almighty had done creating Corrib and Mask and all the other fine big loughs of Ireland, He then had to make people to fish on them. To achieve this He must first have shaped three moulds, one for the trolling man, one for the dapping man and one for the fisher of flies. The trolling man turned out broad in the shoulder with a distinctly hunched appearance, the dapping man carried more flesh and made excellent ballast in the boat, and the fly-caster was more lithe than either and much quicker in reaction. Of course, in the long chain of evolution, many of us have become pure hybrids, multifarious fishermen.

Lough Mask has now become firmly established as the venue for the annual World Cup Wet-Fly Trout Angling Championships, and 1985 witnessed the 21st running of this event on these waters. From fairly modest beginnings of 80-90 rods in the early years, the reputation and popularity of these championships have grown steadily, and a new record of 371 anglers, from many countries, competed in 1985.

A fly-fishing competition that supports such a grandiose title has to be something special, and this one certainly qualifies. A combination of two factors—one of the world's great wild trout waters and skilled boatmen—makes for a promising enough beginning, and many of the boatmen are truly colourful characters, to fish in whose company is an experience in itself. Not only do they know the lough like they know the way upstairs, but the fact that they are themselves competing each day for the Best Boatman prize ensures that they will work hard for their fishermen. Boatmen and anglers are all there to win.

Add to this—excellent administration running throughout the whole event, the best of Irish hospitality and the kind of 'crack' that only the fellowship of anglers can generate—and you begin to get the feel of Cushlough Bay, Ballinrobe, at the start of August.

The championships are now run over five days, the first four of which (Thursday-Sunday) being qualifying heats and leading up to finals day, which is always fished on the Bank Holiday Monday. (In Eire, still the first Monday of August). A maximum of a quarter of those who fish in the heats will qualify for the finals, but only those weighing-in fish will be eligible to go forward, and no competitor may take part in more than one of the qualifying heats. Throughout the competition each boat will carry two anglers—the partnership being decided by draw—but every attempt is made for visiting anglers, new to Lough Mask, to fish alongside locals. The allocation of boatmen is likewise made by draw. Boatmen can compete themselves, but are not allowed to fish on those days when they are acting as boatmen. The great thing is to qualify.

On each of the five days the boats leave from Cushlough at 11.00am and must be back inside the marker-buoy by 6.00pm. It is a thrilling sight, once the start signal has been given, to watch the boats manoeuvre from the stages, then tug their engines into life, as they begin to thread with caution down the narrow channel that leaves the bay, before finally opening up the throttle. Now the whole armada splits, furrowing the lough with long trails of foam as each heads in hope for the chosen ground—a kind of water-borne version of a Red Arrows' display. Such is the upheaval that one wonders any trout will rise at all, and it is certain that the Cushlough drift, at least, will be ruled out for some time.

At 6.00pm we will soon discover how many of those hopes have been fulfilled. The weigh-in is conducted with commendable speed, efficiency and a bonhomie that flows with the general banter. Anglers with fish to weigh string them all together, attaching the label that has been provided, and hand them in. All must be brown trout of 12 inches or over and, once weighed and recorded, these are then returned to their captors. The final results for the day, together with the names of those qualifying for the finals, are then determined by computer.

Over recent years water engineering work—the same work that ruined the lovely river Robe—has called for a measure of limited stocking—only as a temporary policy—and this introduced a new element to the competition. Some fishermen chose to concentrate on the stock fish, believing that they would be easier to catch. Thankfully, all such stocking has now ceased and Mask has reverted to what it should always be—a wild fishery. Of the 260 fish taken in the '85 championships no more than six were stockies; in such a large water the survival rate was always poor anyway. Fortunately, Mask needs no such artificial aids, the natural feeding and spawning facilities being sufficient. Mr Denis Kelleher, the PRO on the World Cup Committee, tells me that two of the rivers currently have an over-spawning problem, and here it is planned to trap and remove some of the surplus fish, strip them, hatch the eggs in the hatchery and in due course return them to the streams.

July is not one of the better fly-fishing months, for the trout start feeding then on the annual bonanza provided by the perch fry, but, as this falls off, so the fly comes into its own again. The average weight of all trout weighed-in in 1985 was 1 lb 5½ oz with the best at 3 lbs 14½ oz.

The championships abound in glorious uncertainties, all adding spice to the general excitement and providing anglers with plenty of good stories.

A few years ago now, Bill Scorer was coming in at the end of finals day and there was still not a fish in the boat. Bright sun and scarce breeze made for poor fishing allround, just the kind of day when bags, if any, would be light, but at least one which put everyone in with an outside, fighting chance. As they started the final drift, Bill's head was buried, peering wistfully into his fly-boxes. He has two great qualities as a fly-fisherman—refusal to give up and an uncanny knack for making inspired, and often outrageous, fly changes. He employed both now and soon his old rod was bending into a heavy fish.

This immediately posed a dilemma for them; to play the fish carefully risked failure to meet the 6 o'clock deadline and an automatic time disqualification; to try and haul him would be equally fraught with danger. Bill, fearing a weak hookhold, chose the way of safety, knowing that, once the fish was in the net, the boatman would motor for the marker-buoy as though he was after Sir Malcolm Campbell himself.

As things turned out, the trout, in the 3 pound plus class, fought long and gamely until deciding, just inches from the net, that glory was not for him. With one shake of the head he was gone, taking with him Bill's chances of the World Cup and also a brand new motorcar.

Such competition fishing is not for me. I have nothing against it in principle; it is only that the art I learnt as a boy I now pursue for relaxation. It is my way of easing the tensions that build up, restoring the harmonies and finding wholeness where waters softly lap. If I wanted the high pressure stuff, it would not be to Ireland that I would go but to the gaming-tables of Las Vegas. All the same, it is still a pity that Bill lost his motorcar.

Before leaving the subject of Mask, I record two dapping stories, both of which took place there—the first on our camping expedition in 1973 and the second when Bill was on his own. The subject of dapping itself is treated in a later chapter.

The hero of the first story is none other than the humble bluebottle or blowfly—call him what you will—and, though he sports no claim to be a classic dapping bait, he can nonetheless prove himself a very deadly man for trout, and he certainly has his day. Bill had known this all his life, for, as a lad in the English North Country, he had learnt his fishing on the many little rills and becks that run among the hills there. He grew to know their secret places—deep holes beneath the bushes, where the dark waters had, in times of flood, eaten their way in under banks. These provided the most desirable residences in the streams and were occupied by the best trout, who grew fatter each summer as the breezes blew many insects onto the water from the boughs above. In such sanctuaries, though a worm or minnow trundled down the run might reach them, they were generally safe enough from the angler's fly.

With cat-like tread Bill had stalked these trout until he could just manage to poke his rod-tip through the branches and lower a natural bluebottle onto the water. Being only feet away from the quarry, this kind of fishing demanded great skill, perfect judgement and the patience of Job, as entanglements were frequent, to say nothing of the difficulties involved in landing a fish, once hooked. It was, nevertheless, an excellent school, for those who can winkle out trout by such methods can surely catch them anywhere.

The bluebottle, of course, has earned himself a thoroughly bad name, and most people regard him as no more than a pest and a threat to the hygiene of the kitchen. He rouses up that killer instinct which is never far below the surface in any of us, though I sometimes wonder if those perfumed sprays, which the housewife now uses, are not more harmful still. Whether we like him or not, he remains a creature of great beauty, whose irridescent, green-blue body reflects like a jewel with the glint of sunlight upon it. Boyhood forays apart, we had neither of us thought seriously about the bluebottle from a fishing point-of-view until it happened more or less by accident.

Nearing the end of our week's fishing holiday, we decided one warm evening that we would go into Ballinrobe for our dinner, to give ourselves a break from the chores of cooking in the tent. Except for one other guest, we had the dining room at the Railway Hotel to ourselves and, with the meal finished, were taking our time over coffee and enjoying a cigar. The hotel waitress, presumably also enjoying a quiet evening, had not yet removed our dirty dinner plates, which soon attracted a large bluebottle, whose appearance must have kindled former triumphs in Bill's mind. After paying our bill, we left the hotel, taking with us two bluebottles in a matchbox.

We had completely forgotten about the wretched creatures when we set out on the lough next morning, where the trout proved hard to move; two undersized fish were all we took in the first two hours. We had just started a new drift down a shore not very far from the entrance to Caher Bay, when Bill looked for a match to light his cigar, and suddenly remembered that the box in his pocket had other tenants.

The wind was fine for dapping and patches of sunlight were starting to penetrate the clouds; if there was ever a time to fish the bluebottle this was it. Bill changed rods and was soon dapping with the first of our two bluebottles. On the top of a rolling wave and against the vast expanses of the lough, it looked absurdly small, but, even at the distance he was fishing it, we could see the radiant splendours of its colours. Then, within minutes, a small circle showed on the wave's crest where the bluebottle had been riding—so quietly did the trout take. Bill did all the right things, lowering his rod-point, allowing plenty of time and was soon playing a handsome fish, which was safely boated.

Now he passed the rod to me, remarking curtly as he did so, 'Your turn, and remember we've only one left, so don't go messing things up.'

This second and last bluebottle produced what was virtually a repeat performance, bringing me a fine $2\frac{1}{2}$ pound trout, which appeared to be an identical twin to the one we already had in the boat. A pair of blowflies from the dirty dinner plates, a glimpse of sunshine, twenty minutes fishing time and 5 pounds of trout—that was not bad going.

We then landed for lunch and the search began for more bluebottles, but we never even saw one, and, in any case, I would defy most people to catch one in the open air. Our arrival, however, had attracted the local cows, which soon gathered round to inspect us. The nearest thing we could get to a bluebottle was the cowdung fly and these were there in plenty, but our efforts to catch them were also in vain. Their name betrays their habitat, and all we succeeded in doing was to add a strange new flavour to our sandwiches. Even if we had got one he would not have been the same man at all.

The following day we went back into Ballinrobe just in order to stock up with bluebottles, but had quite forgotten it was early closing, and all the shops were shut when we arrived. We stood and stared longingly outside the butcher's window, where the thickness of a pane of glass was all that separated us from the finest bluebottles one could have wished for. I suppose that was hardly surprising since they must have been feeding on some of the best steaks in all of Mayo. A maggot-farmer would have had to go a long way to find breeding stock of this kind of quality.

Perhaps it was just as well the shop was closed, for it is one thing to enter a butcher's and ask for meat, but probably quite another to ask for the blowflies only. One man's shame can be another's gold, and, as we headed out into the lough, we carried no such gold. It was, of course, our final day, and one which the sun kept breaking through to gild, as if to tantalize still further the fishers of the humble bluebottle.

The second story relates the capture of a big Mask trout on the dap, though by means far removed from anything that could be described as normal dapping practice. There were four in the boat at the time, a solicitor and his wife from Dublin, Bill Scorer and Tom Duffy, who was the boatman. The solicitor was seated in the bows and fishing traditional wet-flies with Bill doing the same from the stern position; Tom Duffy had the centre seat from where he could control the drift, and was at the same time managing to fish the dap; the solicitor's wife was the only one not fishing, and seemed quite content to recline on the floor of the boat and read her book. Tom was fishing a combination of baits—often referred to in Ireland as 'The Cocktail'—which, in this instance, was a daddy-long-legs and a grasshopper together. Ths silence that prevailed in the boat was a mark of the concentration all four were putting into the job in hand, and the boatman was the first to break it.

'Bejasus', shouts Duffy. 'Just look at that great fish starin' at me dap.'

There, about a foot below the surface, they could all see quite clearly the dark green head of a massive trout as he lay motionless beneath the dap. He appeared totally mesmerized by it, unable to believe his eyes. The daddy/hopper combination is, after all, a most unusual courtship, never intended by nature, so the trout had some justification for his strange behaviour. Anyhow he made no move to take it, and all the time the boat was drifting closer and closer to him. Duffy could do nothing except recover his line and keep the dap on the water, so he called again:

'Bill, cast yer flies over 'im, quick now.'

That really should have been the end of the matter for one of two things was going to happen: either Bill's cast would cross Tom's dapping line or else he would put the big fellow down for good—or possibly do both. Duffy, however, insisted and Bill managed to get his tail fly, a Mallard and Claret, over the fish, who never batted an eyelid, and would not have done so even if he had had one to bat. He just kept on staring. By this stage the boatman's rod was nearly vertical, with the dap and the fish almost at the boat's side. Duffy's next instruction was, if anything, even more unlikely:

'Come on, Bill, whip the net in under 'im.'

Now I know Bill to be a pretty fair operator where the net is concerned, and on more than one occasion he has landed salmon for me, which have been too big to fit into it—sweeping with a deft, curving movement he has got the head and shoulders of the fish—the weighty part—to fold into the meshes, leaving the tail-end protruding. He always makes his own landing nets from string that has been well-soaked in linseed oil, which is then tied to form the meshes and fitted to a collapsible ring of steel, the whole becoming rigid when screwed into the handle. This one had a long, hazelwood handle which he had cut out one afternoon whilst playing cricket. He must have been fielding deep in the country at the time, patrolling the boundary with one eye on the game and the other on the hedgerow behind him.

Bill inserted the net quietly, reaching it well into the water behind the fish. Then, with the trout only inches from the boat, he scooped and held it hard against the boards. In a flash Duffy's fist was over the side, and one magnificent trout lay on the floor of the boat, all four-and-three-quarter pounds of him.

By now it had come on to rain and they decided to pull onto an island for shelter and lunch, where smoke, curling through the trees, told them that another boat was already brewing tea. This one had failed to move a fish all morning and the occupant, a well-known Dublin surgeon, came across to find out how

Duffy's boat had fared, when he spotted the great fish lying on the boards:

'What a grand trout you have', says the surgeon. 'What did you take him on?'

Now Tom Duffy was never the man to tell a lie, so, with his face as straight as a die, he replies,

'Well, sorr, 'ee were fishin' the Mallard and Claret . . . so 'ee was.'

Chapter 8

The Land of the Rosses

It was in the early sixties that I first arrived in the busy little town of Dungloe, self-styled capital of the land of The Rosses, a wild and exceedingly beautiful region that lies on the mid-west of Co Donegal. For twenty consecutive seasons I returned there every summer, like a migrant bird, and found the people amongst the most open-hearted and friendly of any in the country, as well as fishings of a seemingly infinite variety just waiting to be explored.

This was the land that had nurtured both Red Hugh O'Donnell, the fiery warrior and great Irish chieftain, who had ruled the north west region of Tyrconnell at the end of the 15th century, and, more importantly by far, the gentle Columbcille (Dove of the Church).

Saint Columba belonged to that period in history when the lamps of faith, education and learning were going out all over Europe until only Ireland kept the light. He was born in 521 within sight and sound of the lovely Lough Gartan in the green hills of Donegal, with the royal blood of Ireland coursing in his veins. A stone commemorates his birth, and any who sleep upon that stone will be spared the pains of home-sickness: many a sad and sorrowful journey has been made on the eve of exile to this stone of Ráith Cnó. In 563 Columba left Ireland to found a monastery on the little Isle of Iona, that was to bring Christ to the Scots, and thence, via Lindisfarne, to the north of England. For nearly three centuries it became the most famous seat of learning and piety in all the Celtic lands.

Dungloe, like many another Irish town, consists almost entirely of one main street, which runs downhill from the head of the town where the church is, crosses the little river at the bottom and climbs again to the police barracks at the other end. Between church and barracks are many shops, one of the most significant being the large Co-operative Stores, known to all as 'The Cope'. This was started by Paddy Gallagher, a local man, who became one of the pioneers of the Irish Co-operative Movement, that was destined, against all the odds, to bring to an end the power of the 'gombeen' men, who for too long had milked the peasant people dry. To the wretched poverty of the folk inhabiting these brown boglands and jejune pastures, he brought prosperity and a new measure of self-reliance. Unlettered though he was, his achievement is chronicled in his own autobiography, *My Story*, by Paddy the Cope, and very readable it is, full of the courage and humour and simple kindness of the countryfolk, it is no less the story of the Irish people beginning to take their destiny into their own hands.

I was making my way to Sweeney's Family Hotel, whose coat-of-arms adorns the glass portico that juts out onto the pavement in the centre of the town. A doctor with a practice in Lancashire had told me that he had spent a night there and that the proprietor, Mr Sweeney, was 'a very dacent man'. Dessie Sweeney more than fulfilled that description, and ran a very decent hotel too. It was typical of the best kind of Irish country inn, before these began to succumb to the temptations of modernity. The accommodation was simple, comfortable and homely and the place furnished with some fine old pieces. Bright flowers from the garden were everywhere, and the atmosphere one of old-world charm.

It was built like a fortress in the four sides of a square, enclosing a courtyard, which led through an arch onto the main street. Beyond this and approached through another arch lay a bigger yard, where cats and chickens played hide-and-seek amongst the visitors' cars, and Uncle Stan brought in the cows for milking. Here too on top of a tower stood an ancient weather-vane, always a vital indicator to be studied carefully after breakfast, for, with so much water to choose from, the wind direction was often the key factor in deciding where to fish. On the first floor, long corridors ran down three sides of the square, giving access to the bedrooms. Splendid Victorian prints of ancient worthies hung on these walls, but the real master of the landing was a fine gillaroo trout that Dessie had caught on Lough Melvin, or maybe it was Mask.

In addition to the hotel, Dessie also managed an adjacent general store. Such was his nature that he saw to it that even the very poorest people, who came in from the surrounding country, did not go hungry. Both he and Kathleen, his wife, were highly respected and played leading roles in the life of the community. Dessie was a man of many parts, which included acting as a referee for the Gaelic football, and he was always called upon to control the 'local derby' game of Dungloe versus Gweedore. So hard was this match contested, and so fierce the rivalry, that the Archangel Gabriel himself would have been pushed to handle it, but Dessie stood no nonsense. I once watched a derby game which he brought to a summary conclusion, after issuing final warnings to both sides; at the next outbreak of hostilities Dessie caught the ball with some style and marched firmly off the field.

Above all else he loved his fishing. Wednesday was early closing in the town and, once the shop was locked, Dessie would pick up his rod and net and trusty 'Seagull' engine, don his cap and head for the white-trout loughs. I was often privileged to fish with him on these afternoons. He had his own pattern of fishing and fairly rigid tenets, one of which was that you should fish the flies slowly for brown trout and faster for the white-trout. One may not have agreed with all his theories—fishermen seldom do—but Dessie nearly always came in with fish to show.

Bill Scorer was out with him one afternoon and began to dap—Dessie always fished the wet-flies—and was soon bringing up one big fish after another to his 'hoppers', missing every one of them: Dessie fair rocked the boat with his laughter. It was a very great sadness to the whole community, as well as to many others from further afield, who counted him amongst their friends, when in 1972 he died before his time. He was a very dacent man. May God rest his soul in peace.

At that time Sweeney's Hotel was the centre for the local fishing, and had been so for many years. Dessie himself had fished The Rosses for as long as anyone, and knew the varied waters well. He also understood the particular needs of fishermen and could sympathize with their peculiar foibles. Many an evening in those early years we would get back long after the dining room had closed, perhaps returning from some lough, buried distant in the hills, or because a late stir had started to move the fish. Whatever the reason or the hour, we would be made welcome in the kitchen, and nothing ever seemed too much trouble for Annie, who cooked there for many years. Despite our feeble, and not very sincere, protests she soon had the steaks sizzling on the Aga and our wet clothes strung out to dry above the range. It was hardly the kind of practice that was likely to be taught in the Dublin schools of catering, but I know one thing for sure—it brought clients back year after year, and I know at least two fishermen who came back to Dungloe for fifty seasons. In fact, to return to Sweeney's after a long day's fishing was not like coming back to a hotel at all, much more like returning home.

The Rosses, like the west of Ireland generally, is entirely bogland; that is, country resting on top of a deep peat mould that overlies a granite stratum underneath, factors which combine to give the waters their familiar dark colour, and render them acidic and of low pH content. These are the waters which the white-trout favour, making the regions a homeland of famous fisheries, many of which also provide spawning grounds for salmon. The Rosses fishery contains some one hundred and thirty loughs—even this may be a conservative estimate—and, within it, those waters which the white-trout and salmon run, are clearly defined.

The nature of the waters hardly favours the brown trout at all, for, although they are present in almost all the loughs in vast numbers, there is little enough feeding for them and they remain a stunted breed—it is nothing unusual to return thirty or more in a day's white-trout fishing, and not one will make 4 ounces. By the same token they can keep a young novice fly-fisher happy all day long; one such youngster, fishing for these small brownies for the first time ever in a junior competition, hooked a fine white-trout just where the river entered Dungloe lough. Unfortunately for him, that fish only stayed long enough to give one majestic leap, but that lad will remember him as long as he lives.

Although the brown trout situation in these acid waters is generally as I have described it, it is not universally so. There are a few loughs which have no trout in them at all, others where the average size is such as to provide worthwhile fishing, and a few where really good fish may be taken. These last are the 'quare' places, and those who know them guard their whereabouts jealously.

Some waters, however, are nameless, being little more than bogholes, and the fisherman may safely disregard them—that is unless he happens to be 'in the know'. For, sometimes, a man will catch a dozen small trout and let them go in these places, returning in a season or two on a warm summer's evening to smoke his pipe and watch the surface of the pool. Take Brockagh, for example, a pleasant little townland, lying off the beaten track in the hills to the east of Dungloe. It was Eamonn Sweeney who told me a story about Brockagh as we drank one night in the hotel bar. Eamonn, no relation of Dessie's, is one of several talented brothers, all of whom were born in Dungloe, but now scattered widely, except for 'Dodo' who is the doctor there. Each August they return, like the swallows, to the place of their birth, when the whole town seems to have a thin covering of them.

As Eamonn told it, a shepherd was sitting by one of the bogholes, when he noticed a big, black beetle crawling on top of the heather. It must have been the king of all black beetles, he thought, for never had he seen such a huge one before. He watched as it started to climb a shoot of heather, which overarched the water. Seemingly unaware of danger, it reached the point of no return and then tumbled headlong into the black depths below. Fascinated, the shepherd kept his eyes on it as the long, spindly legs flailed the surface, turning the calm into dancing ripples, which spread far. Suddenly, a great swirl broke upon the pool and the beetle was no more to be found.

Later, the shepherd reported what he had seen to Seamus

O'Cnoc. He told him, because all knew him to be a wise old man and teacher of the village. Seamus thought long and hard about the matter, and finally constructed a black beetle of similar proportions, which, when worked on the end of a line, also ruffled the water. Only someone of his wisdom could have devised such a thing, and, setting a large hook in it, he ventured it upon the boghole. Sure enough the great fish came and, after a fierce struggle, Seamus had him on the heather. No-one in those parts had seen such a trout before, but, being the wise man that he was, Seamus removed the hook and gently slipped him back into the dark waters.

Whether Eamonn had drunk too much when he spun me that yarn I really do not know, but Brockagh is just the sort of place where a man might believe such things, and Bill and I know that successors to that mighty fish still swim there.

Fishing a boghole is a science of its own—perhaps more a study than a science. On our last visit there, we sat quietly and surveyed the pool for a long time. Nothing stirred. The evening air, sweet with the scent of hay, was warm; grasshoppers 'sang' in the heather, the buzz of insects all round. It was then we noticed a big fellow move up at the far end. Just as we began to stalk him a local appeared on the scene, and started to engage us in conversation—visitors from the distant world are few and far between in Brockagh. Gazing across the cluster of homesteads and the sweep of hills behind, he complained that the place was becoming 'polluted with deer'—surely a pollution that many Europeans would gladly settle for!

In the course of a season, The Rosses Anglers' Association run several fishing competitions, which always attract a good entry. Various prizes are on offer, including one for the best brown trout that is caught. On competition days many anglers of all ages, once they have clocked in, disappear furtively beyond the distant skylines. No-one knows where they are heading and no-one asks, but always a few lusty brown trout grace the weigh-in. From year to year the whereabouts of success are never broadcast and the mountains and glens of The Rosses keep their secrets.

In times when so many of our fishing waters are of necessity circumscribed and highly ordered—park in the right place, pay your money, sign the sheet, obey the rules—it is good to know that places still exist where a man may set off for the hills to prospect on loughs, virtually unknown and unfished, for the gold they may contain. The sense of exploration and the thrill of new discoveries bring a heightened satisfaction to the energetic angler with an adventurous disposition. Such fishings in The Rosses have about them an essential quality of ruggedness, that blends admirably with the terrain, and it is likely that most of the loughs worth fishing will only be reached by considerable effort. Success, if it comes at all, has to be wrested from the day.

Bill has the ideal instrument for this purpose—a small, lightweight, fibre-glass boat with just enough room for two rods to fish from it. This is towed by car on its trailer as far as the bog-road will allow. When this finally peters out, we lift it off the trailer and start to haul and push it, sometimes for long distances, across the top of the scrub-heather until it can be launched on unsuspecting waters.

Other loughs that produce fair trout-fishing lie closer at hand and amongst these are Alec More, Lough Anure and Mullaghderg. When I first fished Alec More, I used to meet up with Alec Murphy, who often came down in the evenings for a few casts from the shore, once the cows were milked. He loved his fishing almost as much as he loved playing the fiddle, for which he was renowned. Alec had started young Kevin Bonner fly-fishing, a red-headed fourteen-year-old who lived on a small-holding overlooking the lough. Once, when I saw him fishing from the shore, I pulled in and invited him to join me in the boat, and from that time we spent many happy days on the lough together, whilst he was still at school. I came to know the whole Bonner family well, and they told me of the evening when young Kevin had run all the way home from the lough, arriving breathless and in tears, after a long fight with a mighty fish that had finally broken free. Alec Murphy had similar tales to tell.

Though I have caught trout of a pound on Alec More, I have never hooked a larger fish, and still wonder what these big fish were. Alec and Kevin believe that they were white-trout, and it is just possible, because a trickle of a stream does link it to the sea in Traighenagh Bay; they could also have been over-sized trout, ones that were on the way to becoming ferox. Alec More does, however, have a small brother lough lying only three hundred yards away, which is known as Alec Beg. 'More' and 'Beg' in Irish mean 'Big' and 'Little', and both loughs were named after Alec Murphy's grandfather. I know that Little Alec holds white-trout, for I have caught them there, and was broken on one occasion by a really heavy one. A tiny stream runs from Big Alec into Little Alec, but it enters the smaller lough by means of a waterfall that is all of 15 feet, and no white-trout would be able to jump it. Little Alec has its own connection to the sea, a narrow rivulet, scarcely 2 foot across, which the white-trout run, but it is very vulnerable to the poachers' nets, which are far too common in these parts.

Lough Anure is one of the largest and perhaps the most beautiful of all the many loughs in the land of The Rosses. Its name means the 'Lough of the Yew Tree', and derives from the fact that this tree grows on the largest of its islands. It stands in a Gaelic-speaking region, where, in summer, school-children from many parts of Ireland come to lodge in local homes and improve their Irish. On a good day the trout rise freely here, and there is always the offchance of a grilse or a white-trout. On my best day there, when I was out with the late Paddy Boyle as my boatman, I came in with three white-trout to go with my sixteen brownies of above average size.

Mullaghderg lies in the north of The Rosses, hard by the sea and close to Kincasslagh. It is quite different in character from the previous two, sand-based, less rocky and containing large areas of reeds and beds of weed. The first time Bill and I fished it, we called on Senator Sheldon, a member of Dáil Eireann (The Irish

Parliament), who lived beside it and was kind enough to lend us his boat. We knew the trout to be of excellent quality and possessed of a light golden hue, due no doubt to the sand on which they lay, but the senator said that they could be hard to locate at times. He indicated the area of the lough that we should search and wished us well. For the first hour and a half we rose nothing, and then were simultaneously into three fish together. They appeared to us to have a tendency to shoal.

A dry-fly fished close to the weed-beds on a warm evening can also be productive here. It looked just the kind of water that might easily have a late evening hatch of sedges, and, following a warm day, Bill and I set out one evening hoping to find it so. As the sun dipped, the air took on a distinct chill and we knew that the season was too far spent for sedges.

Westwards from The Rosses the Atlantic Ocean reaches out as it stretches for America, its grasping fingers interrupted only by small islands, whose contours hold the last rays of the setting sun. On one such island, the Isle of Aranmore lying seven miles north west of Dungloe, there stands a quiet water, Lough Shore, which I try to visit at least once whenever I am in the region. It holds a special fascination in my mind, so that my journey becomes a kind of pilgrimage to a place that I believe to be unique. Its occupants are wild rainbow trout and there is not a single brown trout in it. It is possible that the ancestors of these fish were introduced there way back in the past, but there is no local knowledge that this was ever done: it is equally possible that they are indigenous stock and, if so, this would certainly make the little lough unique.

Today, of course, most people are familiar with the rainbow trout, for it is the one that the fishmongers display, as well as the one that forms the major part of the stocking policy on the 'put and take' fisheries. The story, however, of its introduction to British waters, dating back a hundred years now, together with its fluctuating success rate is thoroughly confused. This is due to the interbreeding of two distinct sub-species, both of which originate in America. One of these is the steelhead (*salmo gaidneri irideus*), which comes from the west coast of north America: this is essentially a migratory trout, whose life-style is comparable to that of our own sea-trout. The other is the American rainbow trout (*salmo gaidneri shasta*), a native of mountain rivers in the Sierra Nevada: this is much less migratory in habit and, in this respect, resembles more closely our own brown trout. Both strains have now become inextricably crossed.

There are some places in Europe where free-living populations of rainbows have become established after stocking—certain rivers in Austria and Yugoslavia and the River Derwent in Derbyshire are examples, but most attempts to establish local breeding populations continue to fail. Those rainbows, whose descent gives them a predominance of the hereditary character-istics of the *Shasta* strain, will be those most likely to produce free-living stocks: where the steelhead influence predominates this will not happen. The rainbow, as we know him in Britain, is a thoroughly mixed-up, frustrated sort of fellow, who knows neither his proper Mum nor his proper Dad.

To reach the island, an unscheduled open-decked boat leaves the busy fishing station of Burtonport whenever it is ready, and in the summer that is fairly often. Aranmore is a friendly, inviting little isle, some four by two-and-a-half miles in size, and contains a thriving, contented community of small farmers and fishermen. From the point of landing one crosses it by the track that leads steeply up to the lighthouse at the end of the north western peninsular. Here are fine cliffs, where the Atlantic roars below as it rolls in and out of the sea-caves at their base, on the top of which one walks on grass as perfect as any lawn, cropped close by sheep and countless rabbits.

The lough itself lies beside the track, sheltered from the worst of the weather by a gentle tuck of the hills, a mile and a half short of the lighthouse. It has a stony bottom, and being shallow, one can wade well into it. The fish rise freely and give fine sport for the half pounders and above that they are. There are bigger ones (in the 3 lb bracket), and to catch these one needs to be on the water in the late evening as the sun is going, but with a boat to catch, it will be time to pack away the rod before then. In the bag upwards of half a dozen trout, but all of them special fish from this little lough of the far west, plump little *Shastas*, their flanks lined with a band of rich purple (hence the rainbow), and the dark spots continuing into the tail.

We are told that God first set His rainbow in the clouds to be a continuing reminder of His unfailing covenant with man and, through man, with every living creature. As one starts the homeward trek, the islanders will be bringing in the cattle, the fishing boats returning and, across the sea, The Rosses bathed in evening sunlight. With such harmony and beauty at every turn the mind has time to ponder many things, and peace enfolds all.

A marine biologist may confute me, but, until that time, I for one shall go on believing that the rainbows of Aranmore have been there since rainbows have been anywhere.

It was, however, neither the brown trout nor the bright shastas of Aranmore that summoned us back to The Rosses, but the more romantic white-trout. This was the fellow that, though he had shared his youth with the hungry brownies, who knew no better or were seemingly content to struggle for survival in the barren waters that nature had provided, now parts company with them: not for him the meagre pastures of the homestead. His adolescence completed, strange new urges, springing from his ancestors, start to move within him and, obedient to them, he quits the loughs and little connecting rivers and drops down to the sea, where fresh perils and adventures lie in wait. Here he finds an abundant larder and grows strong and lusty. Then, in the second or third weeks of June, he returns and begins to nose his way up the dark threads of rivers, and through loughs, to spawn a new generation in the ancient nurseries, which the mountains guard.

The main white-trout system in The Rosses lies above the little Dungloe river and comprises a chain of loughs that include Dungloe, Tully, Cushkeeragh, Namuck, Fad, Meenlecknalore and Salagh. There are other briefer systems as well as individual loughs, into which the white-trout run, and some loughs, notably, Lough Anure, the Nacung loughs and Owenamarve, will hold salmon as well.

To the fisherman who has laboured on these waters each one reveals its own characteristics, its peculiar ambience; they are as individual and different as folk, and every bit as fickle, sometimes coy as maidens, at others austere as monks, just occasionally uninhibited as revellers. You need to catch them in the mood. Dungloe is often dour—we know her as 'Heartbreak Dungloe'— yet can often spring surprises. Late one afternoon, when the wind had died completely, I saw her entire surface boiling with white-trout, something I have never seen elsewhere. Meenlecknalore is more magnanimous, whilst still remaining her enigmatic self, whereas little Salagh, her shy sister, garlanded with lilies, is simply magical, but all too brief. For me, at any rate, Tully is the jewel in this particular crown, tucked low to the bosom of her founding hills, which furnished her with many faces, she is the most secretive, always enticing, always beguiling, one to be wooed with infinite patience. In a fold of the hills, above her shores, the red throated divers nest each year; winging high above our boat, with necks outstretched, they hail us with a throaty 'Kwuk, Kwuk, Kwuk', a wild and haunting cry that echoes the surge on far-off, sea-washed reefs.

On all these loughs, as on any white-trout lough, the single passport to success is dogged perseverance.

A dinner given in Sweeney's Hotel in 1965 was to usher in a whole new era in the life of this fishery. Apparently much of The Rosses lay in the ownership of the Earl of Mount Charles, whose seat is at Slane Castle in Co Meath, and Dessie paid him an annual rent, albeit a peppercorn one. Dessie, together with the late Pa O'Donnell TD, a much loved and respected lawyer, who for many years represented the region in the Dáil Eireann, invited Mount Charles over for a reception and dinner in the hotel, in the course of which it transpired that he was quite unaware of being the owner of the land or the waters. From all accounts the evening passed in great joviality.

Pa was also an ardent fisherman, who loved nothing better than to be drifting with his boatman down the long reaches of Tully, his eyes fixed firmly on a dapped daddy. He and Dessie were natural leaders in the district, and over the next few years were to do much for the fishery. Already they had schemes in mind for its revival, but these depended upon the Earl's approval. By the end of the evening Mount Charles had readily agreed to hand over the fishings, which he never knew he had, on condition that the waters be available to all and charges kept to a reasonable minimum.

And so was formed The Rosses Anglers' Association which soon gathered to it a band of dedicated local anglers, ready and willing to devote their time and energies to restoring the fishings to something of their former glories. Under Dessie's chairmanship, regular meetings took place, financial grants were sought and obtained from Bord Fáilte (The Irish Tourist Board) and others, schemes of work were discussed and put in hand and a thorough and systematic programme of restoration initiated.

Throughout the next few years they constructed fish passes, sluices and gates to control the levels, steadily improved the many spawning grounds, stocked with thousands of eyed ova from the nearby hatcheries at Glenties and planted trees and shrubs on most of the main islands in the loughs. They also commissioned detailed surveys of certain selected loughs, to be carried out by scientists from the Inland Fisheries Trust (now the Central Fisheries Board), built new boats, improved the mooring facilities and access roads to them, and even went so far as to put up simple huts on the major islands, so that anglers could take their lunch in comparative comfort on days of rain.

I doubt if any fishery has ever been blessed by such a stalwart group of devotees, men like Jim Sharkey (known to all as 'County'), Jamesie Durnion, Donal Timoney, Francie Gallagher and Dave Edwards. There were others too, who worked freely and unstintingly.

Salmon and white-trout are truly wild creatures and, though their habitat in freshwater can always be improved by sympathetic management—the cleaning of rivers and the raking of silted spawning beds and deposition of fresh gravel there—they can never be manipulated.

A photograph, now browning with age, still hangs in the entrance lobby of Sweeney's Hotel which shows a pool on the Clady, which used to be an excellent salmon river, where a single rod once landed twenty-four salmon in a day. It still has a fair run, though nowhere near as prolific as in former years. It flows for some five miles and links the two loughs of Nacung to the sea at Bunbeg, twelve miles north of Dungloe.

In the great days of the river, the old Gweedore Hotel, that had stood beside the road where the river leaves the lough, had been home to many great salmon-fishers over the years. It subsequently fell empty to be ravaged by weather and strangers in the night, and, when I last saw it, only an empty shell remained, the roof had fallen in and the fine wood-panelling was being stripped away. In the whispering silence of its grey walls, however, memories still lingered, and nowhere more vividly than in the mind of Jack Boyd. He had been the principal boatman there, one of the best of the old school, and what he did not know about those waters was not worth knowing at all. Sadly, he suffered a nasty accident in recent years, which caused him to lose a limb, and finally ended his career as a boatman altogether.

1968 turned out to be a very poor white-trout year in The Rosses. I had already returned to England, but Bill was still kicking his heels around in Dungloe. Before returning to Dublin, however, he had met up with Jack Boyd, and decided that he would have one final shot—only this time for a salmon. With the season as lacklustre as it had been, Jack was none too confident about the prospects for salmon, but suggested that Lower Lough Nacung might give as good a chance as any. I owe the description of this outing to a letter I received from Bill, who has never had any pretensions to being a salmon-fisherman, as his account well illustrates.

It also reveals some of the true qualties that belong to the very best boatmen. Irish boatmen, to a man, treat their clients with the utmost respect, even when it is the last thing that they deserve. There are times when a bash on the backside with the wet blade of an oar would be far more appropriate. A fisherman, however, is never told off, even when he is making an almighty hash of things, and advice is given only when it is asked for and, even then, always with deference. I was privileged to go out with Jack Boyd on two occasions only, but they were enough to etch him on my memory as a great boatman. He had, after all, been out with the very best in the business.

On the day of Bill's last fling, Jack reported, as they left the landing-stage, that over six hundred fish had passed through the counter, but with the Nacung loughs two-and-three-quarter miles long and of an average width of around a third of a mile, these were going to take some finding. One did, however, splash at the head of the river to give some sign of hope, though the day was calm and somewhat muggy. Using Bill's engine, they drove to the top of the lough, reaching it as dark clouds began to threaten rain. Bill then tied on the one and only salmon fly in his possession, the one that had risen a salmon to him on Lough Anure the season before. He could sense that Jack was none too keen about the fly, though he would never have said as much in a hundred years. Only when asked for his opinion did Jack venture his reply,

'Well, if you've a confidence in it, sir, then that's better than all the flies ever come out of Hardy's.'
Bill knew that it carried little conviction.

By the time the second drift started, it was raining solidly. A few small brownies had come at the fly, and Jack had given the ancestry of every gentleman that had ever stepped into his boat, including the old admiral—the doyen of them all. Then, all of a sudden, there was a big boil in the lough, followed by a choking sound from Jack and Bill was into a salmon. Not being a regular salmon man, Bill does not reckon to hook them all that often, but on this day he was fishing at his very best; feeling that he had no real title to sport at all, he was out to impress this lover of good fishermen. It was only when the fish took his first jump that things began to go wrong, and badly wrong at that.

A sudden gust of wind now blew Bill's hood right over his eyes, forcing him into a total darkness. In his own words the next few seconds probably saw one of the biggest 'cockups' ever in the long annals of the sport. With the salmon sloshing all over the place, Bill struggled with the hood of his waterproof, the reel and the engine. Enforced blindness brought about a loss of balance, so that he all but joined the salmon in the waters of the lough. Throughout these manoeuvres Jack never uttered a word. It was only when Bill had almost strangled himself in the line that a still, small voice of calm reached his ears,

'When you've that fish under control, sir, we'll try and tow him gently away from those weeds'.

And so they did. Bill played him for another fifteen minutes or so, and Jack netted him with all the ease of a master.

Later that same evening Bill stirred a second salmon, though he never touched the fly, and by this time Jack was becoming just a wee bit interested in that fly himself!

Bill and I, whilst fishing for white-trout on the Irish loughs, have enjoyed several encounters with salmon which, under certain conditions—often a grey day with rain impending—seem quite ready to seize hold of a small fly. Most of these have taken place on Lough Veagh, which lies in the highlands of north west Donegal. Although never a part of The Rosses fishery, it is without doubt the finest white-trout lough to be found in that county. Today it forms a part of the Glenveagh National Park, but, in the days when I knew it, was a private estate in the ownership of the late Henry McIlhenny of Philadelphia, the philanthropist and well-known collector of nineteenth century

French and English paintings. It was through the good offices of Julian Burkitt, his devoted factor for so many years, that I was privileged to fish there once or twice each season. I must have fished it between thirty and forty times now, and have only once failed to come in without a bag of white-trout.

As a lough, it stands supreme and unrivalled in my mind, not just for the quality of its sport, but equally for the savage majesty of the setting in which it lies. It remains a place where profound and intangible powers seem to work upon the spirit with a healing, cleansing balm, and I have yet to pull into the boathouse at the end of a day without experiencing the truth of the psalmist's words:

'Deep calleth unto deep at the noise of thy waterspouts: all thy waves and thy billows are gone over me.'

Perhaps this power and beauty derive from its formation 3,000 million years ago when it lay at the heart of an earthquake zone, which caused the sides of the valley to be pushed in opposite directions, as the earth split along the line of a geological tear-fault, causing much breaking and crushing of rocks. Later still, during the Ice Age, a glacier moved along the line of this fault, gouging out all the weakened areas in its path to form the valley of Glenveagh, a classical rift-valley. Today, one can trace the extent of this erosion in a virtual straight line that runs south-west to north-east, through the valley of the Gweebarra river, Lough Barra, Glenveagh and continuing down through Glen Lough towards the sea.

Lough Veagh itself, some five miles long by half a mile across, lies at the base of this deep cleft, where it is flanked on both sides by steeply-rising mountains: in parts it attains a depth of 40 metres. Remnants of the ancient oak and birch forest still cling to the southern hillsides, whereas the mountains on the opposite shore are much more barren, with the 2,000 foot peak of Dooish falling away dramatically over an ice-carved, rock escarpment to the shores of the lough at its top end. Following heavy rains, waters cascade and tumble in white tongues from these rock-faces, the winds carrying their spray far and wide, conjuring rainbows. Owenveagh river, which runs into the head of the lough, and provides most of the spawning ground for the fish, pursues its brief course down the narrowest neck of this deep ravine.

At the northern end of the lough, the Owencarrow river flows out to run its sluggish course through a boggy valley into Glen Lough, some five miles further down, which in turn runs into the sea at the head of Sheep Haven.

Since 1873 Glenveagh Castle has stood halfway down on the eastern shore, where it is built onto a promontory that overlooks the lough: it is a splendid, castellated mansion, constructed from rough-hewn blocks of granite, and surrounded by superb, sheltered gardens, which are amongst the very finest in Ireland.

The majesty of the whole estate is enhanced even further by the wild creatures that inhabit its moorland acres, and chief of these is the magnificent herd of Red Deer, the largest in Ireland, which roam the hills at will. The twenty-eight miles of fencing, which confine them to the estate, are sometimes breached and descendants of the herd have been found as far south as Sligo. They are skilfully managed and counted annually, which on the rugged terrain is no mean feat: there is also the yearly stag-cull and, beside the lough at the head of Sea-trout Bay, stands the deer bell, which the stalkers toll as a signal to the castle that a boat is needed to ferry a carcase across the water. I once took a salmon off this bell on a Teal and Green, but there was no one to toll it for me then!

I know that places like Glenveagh have a tutelary spirit of their own that broods across their wide expanses, and I have often wondered whence they came, what local alchemies had formed them: invariably the radiations emanating from them are benign and pleasing. No doubt there are some places, whose influence is malign and positively evil, though I have never experienced them, but they will not be the sort that fishermen frequent. Glenveagh has witnessed the cataclysmic powers of nature as well as dire, human tragedy, and perhaps both have played their roles in moulding her protecting spirit.

The estate itself was created by John George Adair, who in 1857-59 purchased several small-holdings, whose tenants at best could only wrest the most meagre of livings from the barren ground. His is a name that still sends a cold shudder through the kindly folk of Donegal, and indeed the whole of Ireland, for the infamous and cruel eviction of all his two hundred and fifty-four tenants during the bitterly cold April of 1861. Their simple homesteads were fired without pity. Adair died in 1885, but his wife, who is remembered for her gentle and generous disposition, survived him by another thirty-six years, and she it was who laid the foundations for the present gardens.

The savagery of that event is still mirrored in the awesome powers that nature can exhibit here. I shall never forget the sight I saw on my first ever visit to fish this lough in the company of Jimmy Connahan, the head boatman. In fact, we were mad to go out at all that day, for it was one of fierce gale and driving rain, but Jimmy was never one to disappoint a gentleman on his first visit, and was quite prepared to row me quietly up the leeshore.

Glenveagh's beauty was veiled, but what we did see was, if anything, even more impressive: towards the centre of the lough a giant fountain of water was spiralling upwards to a height of 20 feet or more, the winds scattering it as far as it reached upwards for the skies, like some demented geyser, an awe-inspiring spectacle of sheer, elemental fury, the like of which I have never seen again on any inland water. The gale was funnelling down onto the lough through the deep, narrow gorges of the mountains, which, by compression, increased its rage, concentrating it on this one, particular spot where both wind and water conspired to produce this seething vortex. Had we ventured within the clutches of its orbit, our frail craft would certainly have been sucked in and swallowed whole. As it was, the little boat furnished us with a box-seat at one of nature's truly grand theatres, where we sat to watch the 'Furies' dance their 'Maelstrom'.

It seemed that the *genius loci* still cherished a memory that reached back to that unimaginable dawn, when the earth's fundament had shattered, the rocks were cleft like timbers and vapours hid the skies. Possibly he was using it now to express his own fury at that outrage when the wind had sighed and, drifting off the mountain, carried on its breath lambent wisps of smoke from the burning hovels of the poor. Wraith-like they wandered the face of grey waters, there to roll briefly on the wave until the lough received them to herself. To the Spirit of Glenveagh—that Ancient Memory—was committed forever the guardianship of a profound and searing grief.

Chapter 9

Dapping the Hopper and Company

143

A grey boat riding the waves of a western lough under huge skies, at either end a pair of hunched figures, their long rods protruding, always reminds me of a miniature warship with fore-and-aft turrets and elevated guns trained to ninety degrees. Such a sight is common enough in Ireland, where dapping is a very popular method of taking white-trout, many locals preferring it to wet-fly fishing. Indeed, if the wind is there, it often fares better, both in the numbers and quality of fish caught.

One cannot describe dapping as true fly-fishing, for no casting is involved, even though, in its purest form, it is fishing the true, living fly, or insect, on the surface of the water. How one rates it as a fishing method seems to be very much a matter of personal inclination. That great Irish white-trout-fisherman, the late Mr Justice Kingsmill Moore, had a deep-rooted antipathy to it, finding the equipment both cumbersome and insensitive. He believed he could do better fishing with a pair of dry-flies, which, instead of confining him to the single, narrow line that the dap must take, enabled him to cover more water, as well as any fish which showed off the course of the drift. He may well have been right, though, given the choice, I would opt for the dap every time. In his fine book, *A Man May Fish,* he describes dapping as the dullest and least skilful of all methods.

In broad terms, I find myself sharing his view, but to a limited extent only, and with very definite reservations. It has its place and its plus side. For one thing it allows a virtual novice, a youngster not yet up to the rigours of a day's casting, to catch a big fish. The sheer excitement of the slow head-and-tail roll, as such a fish turns to take the dap, has proved the launch-pad to many a fishing career.

Successful dapping calls for intense concentration and it is certainly not devoid of skills. Fly-fishers, coming new to dapping, frequently fail to hook their fish, nor are they alone in this; it also happens to lifelong dappers, and more fish are probably missed on the strike than are hooked.

I see dapping as a useful variant in a day's lough-fishing and, provided the wind seems likely to maintain its strength, I always like to set out with the dap available in the boat. It can then be called into use as and when required. It is particularly useful on those days when the fish are down, and the wet-flies return time and again with never an offer. How often does it conjure a big fish up from the depths! These are the days when the casting arm grows weary, and two or three drifts with the dap afford a welcome change. Even if non-productive, one resumes casting with renewed verve, and this in itself may do the trick.

Rods for dapping have been greatly modified over the years. By today's standards those used by the great Irish dapping masters of the past were indeed cumbersome affairs. I have one in my possession, presented to me on my first visit to Ireland by the proprietor of the Corrib Hotel in Oughterard on the shores of Lough Corrib. Perhaps he thought I had the muscle to use it! The two lower sections are of stout bamboo with a tapering greenheart top-piece, which gives the action, almost 16 feet in length and weighing two full pounds. It is certainly a fine piece, though I confess I have never used it, and it remains in my attic: to catch a fish on it would be rather like catching one on an oak tree! Perhaps I should now present it to a museum of fishing antiquities.

Most of today's rods, of glass or carbon fibre, are 12-14 feet. Such lengths make awkward stowage in the boat, especially on a day when one is both fly-fishing and dapping, and for this reason I prefer my 13-foot aluminium, telescopic rod, made by Shakespeare. When not in use it can be collapsed and stowed nicely. But even this weighs half as much as the old bamboo, making it too heavy an instrument for playing the sporting Irish white-trout, and giving little feel for intimate contact with the fish. Bill and I have now abandoned dapping rods as such in favour of our normal 10 foot casting ones with 10 yards of blowline attached to the end of the fly-line. Our normal practice is to set out with our two casting rods, and to share the third one which is already set up for dapping. In any moderate to fresh wind, we can still get the necessary distance, together with all the other advantages of lightness and touch and convenient stowage.

If the traditional dapping rod is used, the tackle is completed with a fly-reel containing 8–10lb breaking strain nylon in place of fly-line, 12 yards of floss or blowline with 4 foot of six pound breaking strain nylon and a size 8 hook. Floss silk line may be lighter than blowline but it has two main drawbacks. Once it becomes wet, it clings like a limpet to everything it touches, including the rod and its rings, and hooks can become hopelessly enmeshed in it. Floss nylon line—Shakespeare marketed one called 'Fish Hawk'—or blowline are preferable.

The baits used in dapping are of two kinds, the natural insect and the artificial. Almost certainly the natural insect will prove the better, not only because it is natural but also because it will be working in the water under its own impulses. The most commonly used of these are the daddy long-legs and the grasshopper, fished either singly or in combination. Both are handsome insects whose size, form and colours attract the interest of the fish, and both are readily collectible—daddies more so than hoppers, although they may not be plentiful until the latter part of the season. I have no doubt that other naturals would also succeed, as they do with brown trout, but Irish angling conservatism rarely ventures into the fields of experiment; with the two faithfuls as successful as they are, the results would be little more than academic anyway.

Of the two, I have a strong preference for the hopper: its more robust structure makes it a far better survivor of the constant onslaughts from innumerable and insatiable small brown trout, which can reduce one's store of baits in a very short time, if allowed to do so. I also have a slinking feeling that the lustre of its greens and yellows, and occasional reds, may in certain conditions of light make it more arresting to the fish than the more sombre browns and fawns of the daddy. A trout views a floating object from below, that is by transmitted light, and, therefore, the more translucent the object is, the more readily it is noticed. This is, however, pure conjecture.

When it comes to collecting the natural dap for a day's fishing the best instrument, without any question, is a young, local boy. Provided he has a couple of day's notice and the expectation of a modest fee, he is usually only too pleased to glean the meadows for a jar-full of daddies or hoppers: familiar fields suddenly become a source of wealth, and, at 5 to 10p per hopper, a little diligent searching can open the way to many ice-creams and other delights. Sharp eyes, fast reactions and a delicate touch are all that is needed.

Warm, dry days when the sun is shining provide the best conditions, for then it is that the daddies are out in force on the whin-bushes, whilst the hoppers 'sing' merrily in the grasses and amongst the heathers. This chirping of the grasshoppers is, in fact, no song at all, but is caused by the rubbing together of the edges of the front wings. My own hearing was somewhat impaired by gunfire, with the result that all sounds that go above a certain pitch are now inaudible, and I have not heard the cry of the bat nor the 'singing' of the hoppers since I was a boy, but Bill is quick to hear them still.

The first boatman I ever had on Beltra—one of the great loughs that lies above Newport in Co Mayo—told me that his two bishops, on the previous day, had run out of daddies by lunchtime, and, as both were dapping men through and through, the pair went off onto the bog to hunt some more. One was pretty skilled and soon had a good collection, but the other was much too ham-fisted, snatching at almost anything that flew past him, and it was not long before his hand closed firmly on a wasp. I think the boatman fully expected that the wasp would do him no harm, just because he was a bishop. Wasps, however, lacking piety, always reject 'the laying on of hands'—even episcopal ones.

'D' yer know what?'' the boatman asked me.

'Yes I do, Paddy, but go on, you tell me'.

'Well, sorr, that wasp, 'ee stung 'is Lordship right below 'is bishop's ring, the unbelayvin' crayture.'

In deference to Mother Church, and perhaps my own cloth, Paddy never told me what that bishop had actually said. 'But 'ee fished terrible bad all afternoon, so 'ee did.'

This particular boatman, who hailed from Castlebar, must have been still suffering from a surfeit of bishops when he took me out. For some reason he had also brought along a young boy, whom I took to be his son and aged about twelve, but the lad showed no interest in the fishing, preferring to sit in the bows and read his comic, his jaws exuding balloons of bubble-gum, which burst upon the ether with explosive venom. As we neared the end of the first drift, I hooked into a good fish—a spark which soon kindled new life into the youngster who now rose to his feet, scattering the pages of his comic, which dropped like autumn leaves, upon the waters, and almost went overboard himself. The man from Castlebar seemed to catch the same fever:

'Hold him, hold him, my lord, it's a salmon.'

In order to calm the situation, for disaster loomed imminent, I replied:

'It's just a white-trout, Paddy: no more a salmon than I'm a bishop.'

Boatmen, of whatever persuasion, seem to excel themselves in the grand titles, especially if they know their fisherman to be 'of the cloth'. On many a first outing of a new season a loud bellow from across the waters falls upon my ears:

'Is that yerself, yer reverence?'

I have seen some very ingenious constructions for storing the daddies, especially in the boathouse on Lough Inagh in Co Galway, a large, beautiful and widely-fished water: these are cleverly designed boxes, consisting of compartments with wire gauze and trap-doors—Heath Robinson in his heyday could hardly have been more contriving. They combine both de luxe, air-conditioned accommodation with a quick release facility, whereby only one daddy emerges at a time, thus avoiding an eight to twenty percent loss each time you take the lid off to extract one.

All such contraptions, however, are for the dapping purists only, and Bill and I are much more down-to-earth practitioners, often having to hunt the hedgerows first to find a suitable container, before going on to collect the hoppers; a narrow-necked jar is best, and old sauce bottles are ideal. The jar should be lined with grasses and provided with ventilation. Once in the boat, it needs to be kept either in the pocket or in the fishing bag, and not left to roll around on the floor of the boat—a sure recipe for disaster: invariably the next time you want a hopper, water will have found its way in through the air-holes, and all will be drowned.

Artificial 'flies', specifically for dapping, originated in Scotland with the famous Loch Ordie patterns, whch resembled large, hairy spiders, and I have seen some that were tied as big as golf balls. They do work in Ireland in a large wave, but are not widely used. Buoyancy is an all-important factor, and the Irish prefer to use one of the large Sedges, the Daddy or any well-hackled Palmer or Bumble-type fly such as the Heather Moth. The clear advantage, which the artificial enjoys, is that it cannot be knocked off by a small fish.

It should be fished in such a way that it skims across the top of the surface, covering an arc both sides of the line of drift: it is this particular movement, coupled with the consequent disturbance of the water, that excites the fish, rather than any ability to represent a particular creature. As a boy beside the river Dovey in Wales, I watched evening sewin rising to thistledown that the wind caused to skim over the surface of the pool—a very similar action to the artificial dap.

Dapping technique is simple enough, and dependent upon fresh to strong winds. With the insect mounted delicately, the blowline is paid out from a raised rod, until the wind catches the light line, billowing it out into a concave curve. Once sufficient line is out, the rod is lowered, until the bait *and nothing else* touches the surface of the water. The insect is then in a correct fishing position, where it rides on top of the wave at the speed and along the course of the boat's drift: in contrast a dry-fly would remain static on the water. Viewed from the side, the sweep of the dapping lines resembles the well-set spinnakers of yachts running before the breeze. A fading wind causes the nylon to drop on the water, and a gusting wind lifts the bait into the sky: the dapper maintains the bait in a fishing position by constant adjustments to the angle of the rod. Concentration is needed all the time.

With floss-nylon it is possible to dap successfully even in a light breeze, but the terminal cast must also be lighter—3 foot of 4lb breaking strain nylon. Very windy days, however, make it difficult to keep the dap on the water at all. The rod now has to be kept low, and this is the time to use a longer cast of heavier nylon—8 foot of 12lb breaking strain—and to fish an anchor-fly two feet below the dap. This can be any heavy wet-fly and, by dragging in the water, serves to keep the dap, now fished as a dropper, on the surface; but keep alert, for sometimes a fish will seize the anchor-fly rather than the dap!

One useful refinement in a dapping boat is a rod-holder that can be clamped onto the gunwhale. All it is is a metal tube, into which the rod-butt slips, thereby keeping the rod vertical, and freeing both hands to change the bait or dry the artificial.

To pick up the dapping rod after a spell of casting the wet-flies involves more than a change of method—a mental change is also needed, for the strike must be entirely different. With the wet-flies it is necessary to tighten into the fish at once, but to do the same when dapping would almost certainly mean losing the fish. The boatman, who first introduced me to dapping on Lough Corrib, advised me to lower the rod-point when a fish came, count to three and then tighten into him. He told me that the finest dapper he ever knew was an Irish missionary priest who worked in Africa.

'The good Father', he said, 'always had time for three *Ave Marias* before he hooked the fish.'

The boatman's instructions were good, basic advice for a beginner; though, with experience, one learns to judge it more or less intuitively.

Dapping's real skill, therefore, lies in this ability to time the strike correctly, and there is no fisherman who gets it right all the time. A filmed sequence of a take, played back slowly, would show a fairly leisured roll, as the fish comes up, takes with open mouth and then goes down to enjoy the meal. The strike clearly has to be delayed until after the fish has turned; to make it in the excitement of the take would only pull the bait straight out of his mouth. They also come at differing angles of approach, which introduces yet another variable to correct timing. The strike must always be quicker with artificials, as these are soon rejected, but slower with naturals—and slower with hoppers than with daddies. In the final analysis, however, it all comes down to experience, and there will be times, as with first serves in tennis, when percentages may be low.

I remember a humbling experience on Lough Beltra, when I was dapping the natural daddy and rose some fifteen white-trout, missing every single one of them. I began by giving them plenty of time, then speeded up and finally struck on sight, but, whatever I did, I just could not hook a fish. My boatman, one of the most experienced on the lough, then told me of the day when he was out with a man and wife, both of whom were capable fishers, and each was dapping from a different end of the boat. The woman took ten white-trout, her husband none and both rose about the same number of fish. There seemed to be no rhyme nor reason in it. Could it have been the angle of the sun? They should really have swopped seats halfway through to find out.

All sorts of interesting combinations can occur in a boat where one rod is dapping and the other casting, and one of these is what I call 'the Combined Operations Fish'. A white-trout that rises to the hopper may well be hooked, but sometimes he misses the bait altogether. When that happens, it is important to keep the dap where it is, for a fish that mis-cues will come looking for it again, and usually takes at the second attempt. At other times, a white-trout manages to clean the hopper, leaving only a bare hook: now is the moment for the back-up party to cast his flies across at once, and eight times out of ten that fish will take again. Bill and I have had several like this over the years. Supposing we were not the best of friends, a fish taken this way might well cause an argument as to who had really caught it, rather as a footballer might claim a goal, even though his shot was diverted off another player. Such a fish is the true prize of a genuine team-work with all services in action.

A grey, windy day is sometimes just the day when a salmon in the lough will move to take a dap, something that I have witnessed on at least four occasions, but we have yet to hook our man. In the early years Bill was always experimenting with dapping baits, and tried almost anything and everything— from large dragonflies to cabbage white butterflies, to hairy caterpillars—until he had exhausted the whole gamut, but no break-through ever came. The first time we rose a salmon, he was dapping the 'Monstrosity', an artificial construction of no known pedigree. The water was Lough Anure and we were out in the late Paddy Boyle's boat: Paddy had now retired from his work, and came as our boatman—there was nothing he loved better than a day on the lough.

That very winter, Bill had been to a sale of sporting equipment, when he had acquired an ancient box of flies, all of which were now at least sixty years old. I was busy casting, whilst Paddy held the boat on drift, and from the corner of my eye could see that Bill was about to make a change, his head now buried in this box of treasures. He then extracted one of the most fearsome objects I have ever seen, huge, round, black and fluffy: to call it a fly would have been absurd, even to suggest it belonged to the Loch Ordie tribe would have been an insult to that famous genus. If it resembled anything at all, it would possibly have been some giant, hairy, man-eating spider from a tropical rain-forest. Bill, at least, must have had faith in its potential, which is all that matters, for he tied it on the end of his line and was soon dapping it on the wave.

Disbelief had rendered poor old Paddy speechless, and it was now left to me to keep up the tone of the boat, if nothing else, by continuing to fish my wet-flies in the hallowed manner. Then, just as the drift brought us close to a rocky shoreline, up came a large, dark head, as a fine salmon rolled on top of the water, like a porpoise, to go down again, taking the monstrosity with him as he did so. Bill lowered his rod-point and, giving the fish plenty of time to complete his roll, tightened, but made no contact. The drift was fast, but Bill managed to return his dap to the water with commendable speed: twice more that fellow came and twice more appeared to take it well, but both results were as before.

The same kind of thing happened on another occasion. This time the two of us were out on Lough Owenamarve, a much smaller water at the head of the system, above the little Derrydruel river in The Rosses. The day had started thoroughly badly with Bill breaking the top of his fibre-glass rod. I would have driven back to Sweeneys for my spare rod, but Bill was content to carry out on-the-spot repairs, whipping on a temporary splint. This lent the rod a measure of respectability, though it was obvious to both of us that it was not going to stand up to much stick, if any at all.

A strong two-pound white-trout, which came at the point where the river enters, was sufficient to undo all his good work and, as casting was now out of the question, Bill decided to go onto the dap. He put up the solitary hopper, which was all that remained in the jar. The wind was strong enough to take the bait out, though the rod looked a sad and sorry sight, its end now drooping forlornly, like the fag in a docker's mouth. This, of course, was the moment Murphy had been waiting for—the circumstances combined to make the operation of his law all but inevitable—and Bill's heart was well and truly in his mouth when a salmon cleaned his hook. The final test of the old rod never took place, and the great fish was happy with his hopper.

Bill is a fine fisherman but, if I were to fault him in any one respect, it would probably be in the maintenance of his tackle. I end this chapter with another sad tale, because it illustrates what I believe to be one of dapping's greatest merits.

The lough in question was Emlough, belonging to the Zetland Fishery in Connemara, at the end of the first week of September, 1986, on a day that was dark and somewhat chill, but by no means hopeless. Three rods, however, hammered away all day without rising a single fish. On the final drift I was acting as boatman, with my two companions casting at either side of me, and decided to put out the hopper, using Bill's dapping equipment, which was already set up. Before leaving Dublin, Bill, thinking his dapping line was suspect, had raided the bathroom and substituted it with dental floss. The manufacturers market this in 50 metre lengths. It is both light and immensely strong—quite impossible to break by hand. I can see no reason why it should not be admirable for dapping, except, that is, that it lost me what I believe would have been by far my biggest white-trout ever.

This fish came very quietly to my hopper and I hooked him well, whereupon he tore off across the lough until, after a run of 50 yards, he was abruptly halted by a reel that jammed completely: the break was instantaneous. I had felt the full weight of this fish, and the surging power of that first run that was far from finished, and am sure that he was in excess of 5 lbs. Bill's somewhat laconic comment was:

'H'mm . . . I suspected that reel was a bit dodgy'.

Chapter 10

Mhin Leic Na Leabhar

The names of Irish white-trout loughs derive from an ancient language, and many of them trip from the tongue with all the whimsical cadences of a true poetry. Who, for example, can venture forth to fish on waters with such names as Shanakeela, Clonadoon or Cappahoosh without the feeling of an ambient mystery pervading the scene all about him? A name is never just a name, a means of identification, a mere convenience, for it contains within it the very essence and nature of the thing itself. Beside the ford of Jabbok, Jacob wrestled all night long with an angel and, as dawn began to break, he asked its name, but it was never vouchsafed. The Jewish people have always held that to know the name of something bestows upon the owner a certain power over that subject—that is why they never knew the name of God: He may reveal to His people certain aspects of His nature, but His name must be forever shrouded by the 'cloud of unknowing'. Let the white-trout fisher, however worldly-wise he may be and sophisticated his technique, pull out from the shore, content only in the mystery itself, for there is an essential otherness there that he may never know.

Not far from Dungloe and within sight of the road that leads to Glenties, there stands a metal pole with a white disc on top, firmly planted in the bog. Some sixty yards below it, and across springy heather that grows above the black, steep walls of old turf-cuttings, lies a small and insignificant lough. Most who pass along that road ignore this pole completely, and even the curious few, who pause to read it, will not be much the wiser, for it bears a strange legend—*MHIN LEIC NA LEABHAR*. For all they know, that could be Irish for 'There's a bull in this field', and they too are glad to hurry on. This little lough, however, despite her unprepossessing appearance, is not without her friends, for there remains a charmed few, a handful of fishermen, whom dogged perseverance and happy chance have fashioned into a select band of cognoscenti. In the early years of our fishing together, Bill and I were initiated into the mysteries of Mhin Leic Na Leabhar through a process of baptism.

At that time the lough was serviced—if that is the right word for it—by an old flat-bottomed boat. Even in her prime she had proved awkward to row, and drifted like an old cow. But now, even that was behind her, and she was already at the stage where the bailing-tin was likely to be of more help than the oars. Knowing this, we had come with our own emergency repair kit, consisting mainly of an ample supply of putty.

On arrival, we found her hull-down in the water, and the attempt to bale her out proved a Herculean task, as new water entered almost as fast as the old was thrown out. By a combination of bailing and tipping, hauling and cursing we eventually got her up-ended and onto the bank to reveal her bottom, which resembled nothing less than a tinker's day-off: patches of tin adhered miraculously, and hung, festooned with trailing arms of weed, against a Dalmatian-spotted background, where blobs of putty had been blotched by dollops of tar. Clearly, we were not the first who had tried to put her right.

To get her fit to satisfy Lloyd's underwriters was quite out of the question, and even to put her into some sort of shape, so that we could fish what remained of the day, was problematical enough. Without her, however, we had no means of covering the fish that lay just off the weedbeds in the narrows of the lough. All we could hope for was to plug as many holes as possible and then, like Agag, to tread delicately. Fortunately, we already knew the lough well enough to have discovered where most of the submerged rocks lay; to have hit one of these in our present condition would certainly have sent us to the bottom. At last, we eased her back into the water and, with our rods set up, gently pushed her out through the weeds and into the open lough.

As if our problems were not enough already, the wind added to them, for it was all wrong for the water. Instead of the favoured south westerly, which would have let us drift the length of the narrows, it was blowing from the south east. The only way we could fish the narrows in this wind was to drift across them, which increased the work-rate and would put more strain on the old tub. In fact, the drift became so short that most would be completed in barely twenty casts, and much of the time we would be crossing again and again those areas we wanted to fish. At the start, the boat seemed to be holding together, but only by the skin of its putty, and bailing had to be continuous. There was no way that Bill and I could fish together, for whoever was not rowing or fishing was acting like a human bilge-pump.

The strange thing was that, although boat and wind conspired against us, the white-trout started to come on with an abandon that in twenty-five years of lough-fishing I have seldom seen repeated. They seemed to sense our discomfort. Each time we crossed these narrows, fish were risen, not in ones but in twos and even threes. It appeared that all they wanted out of life was to catch a sight of a Donegal Blue or a Black Pennell. I know that, had we had a decent boat that day, so that we could have concentrated on fishing rather than survival, we would have come off with a fine bag. Mhin Leic Na Leabhar, meanwhile, had other designs for these late-come shipwrights.

Perhaps it was the speed and excitement of the sport, as much as anything, that in the end proved too much for the ancient barque. The water was now beginning to come in faster and faster, so that even bailing was no longer worth the candle. By the time we started the last drift, all thoughts of damage-control had been abandoned and we were both fishing. The hull gradually dipped lower and lower, timber by timber, as the waters began to swill and lap around our knees; there would be no more drifting after this one. For me, bound as I was for Liverpool the following day, it was the last drift of the season anyway, but for the old flat-bottomed it was to be the final drift of all.

The tradition in the Senior Service is that the captain is the last to leave a sinking ship, but with the white-trout in this mood neither of us thought of leaving; there was nowhere to go to except into the lough and we were heading that way in any case. What the white-trout thought, we shall never know. By the end of August they would have grown accustomed to the dark shadow of a boat as it glided overhead, but this was something different altogether. We must have looked like a submarine coming at them or, more familiar, some kind of land-locked seal, and perhaps this was what had made them so lively. By now we were so full of water that steerage was no longer possible. The drift ended as the boat, three quarters full of water, struck a rock close to the shore, tipping her gunwale beneath the water-line and sending her to her last mooring.

The impact, when it came, caused Bill to lose his rod overboard, a treasured one he had had for many years, given by his father as a prize for passing the Common Entrance exam to Giggleswick School. Though we were not able to recover it then, at least the rock marked its resting place, and over the next day or two Bill and Dessie Sweeney were to spend many hours with grapnels trying to retrieve it. It was only a chance glint of sunlight from the reel that finally brought success, and Bill still fishes with the rod today. As he tells the story of our sinking, he relates that, when the boat was no longer visible, 'Street fished on', and, believing as I do, that there is always time for one more cast, he was probably right in this.

In the years that have passed since then, we have fished these narrows many times, casting our flies and sometimes taking fish from around the fateful rock where our boat lies buried and preserved in the mud and silt of the little lough. Perhaps in the centuries that lie ahead, when fishings as we have known them are no longer possible, our boat may be recovered, like the *Mary Rose*, and lovingly restored by men, for whom trout-fishing now exists only in the literature of the past, to be exhibited as an example of how twentieth century man had once pursued his wild pleasures. Like many another boat on the western fisheries, it may even have a fly or two, adhering to its timbers, to give yet further evidence of a long-lost sport that had provided so much delight to their distant forebears.

With these baptismal rites completed, Bill and I began to feel that Mhin Leic Na Leabhar had embraced us to her bosom and, though her white-trout were never again to show quite the same exuberance, we at least felt that, if we remained faithful, she would in time open her store of treasure still further. 'Meenlecknalore' is the usual name by which this lough is known, but I prefer the one that is on the pole, for it better fits her nature, suggesting, as it does, something that lies on the farther side of human intelligence, full of spirit-power and the mists of Celtic mythology. I know it now to be a place where almost anything can happen and it usually does.

It was here I caught a white-trout as the lightning struck the water and a cloud-burst drenched me to the skin in minutes, and on a gentler day almost caught another which seized the tail-fly, as my rod rested against the gunwale and I was engaged in changing the bob-fly. Here, too, a big fish snatched my Peter Ross, when I was side-casting, whilst Bill rowed quietly through the neck of the narrows. On this occasion I paid the penalty for my own carelessness, for that fish went off with my cast of three flies, and, in my eagerness to set out, I had failed to check a days-old cast before tying it on my line. A notice in the window of Charlie Bonner's shop in Dungloe announced that the best white-trout to date from the fishery was a mere $2\frac{1}{4}$ lbs, and this one clearly had the beating of it.

Mhin Leic Na Leabhar is the sixth lough up on the Dungloe white-trout system, and in shape resembles a smoker's pipe, one end forming a rounded bowl, which is almost divided in two by a line of rocks and small islands. The bowl then tapers into a long stem of narrow water with the river coming in at the mouthpiece. North of these narrows, the land rises steeply and the hill is clothed by an oak grove, a last proud remnant of ancient forest that once thrived. Water and oaks, sites much favoured by the Druids, were long regarded as the home of elemental spirits, and their coming together here further suggests the strange, irrational powers that Mhin Leic Na Leabhar so often displays.

The half-mile length of river, which twists and turns to the very brink of the trees, can all be covered by the boat as the oars dip easily into the beds of lilies, whose flowers in August bob up and down to their stroke, looking like so many fried eggs on large platters of dark green. At its head, the river connects to Mhin Leic Na Leabhar's little sister—Lough Salagh—whose name means the 'dirty lough', and probably so given because this water is even weedier than her bigger sister. Weedy she may be, but she ought never to be missed, especially if the wind is fresh and from the south west, for it is the top one in the white-trout chain. It is true that another lough—Lough Adreen—lies a mile and a half above it, but few fish make their way that far and the river above Salagh is where most fish will spawn in November.

Provided there has been sufficient water to bring them through, tiny, egg-shaped Salagh always holds fish, and by August many of them may have been up for some time. Though these will have lost their silver lustre and begun to darken, they still provide excellent sport, but fresh, bright fish can still be found there. One shore is bordered by a cattle meadow, which rises steeply to the Doochary road where the old National School stands, now converted to a private dwelling. At its head, an arched stone bridge carries the road over the little river that comes from Lough Adreen, which now runs into Salagh through a barrage of reeds, and this is where most fish tend to lie.

I used to imagine that the ideal job would have been that of headmaster of the Salagh National School, and one that could easily have been combined with that of water-bailiff. One would have been admirably situated for this, able to pursue one's didactic calling and keep a watchful eye on the lough from the classroom window at the same time. And what an education the local natural history could have provided, with the whole life-cycle of the white-trout, from the hatching of the eggs to their return to the spawning redds, there before their eyes. The horny-handed sons of toil, who were its scholars, lived their lives midst the ever-changing splendours of The Rosses, and surrounded by so many wild and beautiful creatures. Nor would I have been short of willing hands to round up a jar of hoppers when needed!

The birds and animals to be found beside the loughs are all part and parcel of a day's fishing, bringing their own colours and delight to it; and, as fishermen tend to pursue their sport in sombre dress, quietly and unobtrusively, will often approach quite closely. Of the larger mammals, hares, foxes and badgers are plentiful, though the latter two are seldom seen, except perhaps in the headlights of the car, which is often their undoing, and many fall victim on the roads. Otters too are present, though becoming rare, and the more intrusive mink is much more likely to be seen. On one occasion, when fishing the narrows, Bill and I both heard what sounded like a solid white-trout rise behind the boat, and, on turning round, were surprised to see a pair of mink apparently enjoying a game, as they chased one another across the tops of the rocks along the shore, plunging in from time to time for brief swims.

These feral mink, descendants of ones which escaped from the various mink farms, are now on the official list of British and Irish fauna. They are the first carnivores to be introduced to these islands since we parted company from the land mass of Europe. Like the grey squirrels, they have no natural enemies, unless it be man himself, and both are definitely here to stay. Already they are earning a bad name for themselves for their habits of raiding poultry and for their depredations on the fisheries. Unlike the otter, however, they cannot remain submerged for longer than about fifteen seconds, so their damage to fish stocks is probably not great, although they do prey on the waterbirds.

Field-glasses are always an asset in the boat and on this occasion we had fine views of the mink at play, but on Mhin Leic Na Leabhar I have my eyes open for two other birds in particular. One of these is a hawk, who has his home amongst the oaks and regularly quarters the nearby heath and farmland, but always too distant for positive identification. The many granite boulders make favourite perches for the handsome little stonechats, and, as I set up my rod beside the boat, one takes his stance and, jerking wings and tail, roundly scolds me in harsh, staccato notes. My father, who was no authority on birds, once told me over dinner at Sweeney's that he had seen 'a small bird in evening dress': this puzzled me until I realised that it must have been a cock stonechat—a very fair description too.

Mhin Leic Na Leabhar keeps her secrets yet, only revealing them slowly to her closest friends. I cannot translate her name, nor do I intend to find it out for such probings, or presumption, could just be the breaking of her spell.

Chapter 11

Athry, Gowla and Ghosts in Connemara

A succession of poor seasons in Donegal in the mid-seventies convinced both Bill and me that the overall stock of white-trout there was now in serious decline. Eight full fishing days in 1977, which had included a day on Lough Veagh, yielded us only nine small fish, all of them harvesters, and, though my diary records that conditions were mainly adverse, they had not been all that bad. We decided then that the following year we would seek fresh pastures, and made tentative plans to meet up in Connemara and take our chances there. This was to bring us to the waters of the Zetland fishery which belong to the Zetland Hotel in Cashel.

In the fishery office here, along one side of the wall, hung a fine old map, now somewhat wrinkled and faded by time, but still showing in fair detail the extent of the waters, which embraced two separate systems. One of these, an offshoot of the better known Ballynahinch system, contained the two Athry loughs with Emlough lying above them; the other lay above the Owengowla River and comprised the various beats on the river, together with Gowla Lough, Mannion's Lough, Redman's Lough, White's Lough and Anillaun near the top.

A third system—the Invermore—had formerly belonged to the Zetland but was now in private hands, though permits to fish were readily available locally. This too was, and still is, an excellent fishery, containing many delightful waters, that lay above the Inver river on the road to Screeb. Lough Curreel near the head was, perhaps, the most spectacular of these, containing a handsome stone house, built amongst the pines on its main island. To reach it from the point where the car has to stop, a mile trek leads across the bog, every inch of which had at one time been laid with paving stones, though many are now submerged beneath the turf. The island house is not lived in but still in good repair, and would make an ideal fishing-lodge; its main room contains a fine stone fireplace, carved with the forms of white-trout, and a splendid dining table that overlooked the waters. One shudders to think of the difficulties that had to be overcome to put it there at all, to say nothing of the labourers' rates of pay.

Bill and I soon introduced ourselves to Josie Keany, who was at that time the manager of the Zetland fishery. He was a true enthusiast, who knew his job inside out and whose chief concern was that more real fishermen should fish the waters and do well on them. From a cursory glance at the daily fishing sheets in the office, it was apparent to us that there were not many rods on the waters at all, and the results were far from impressive, a view that Josie also shared; he felt that the fishery was not being put fully to the test. We made up our minds there and then that we would settle for these waters and fish them hard for the next two weeks.

Josie could not have been more helpful, giving us a boat on Gowla for our first day and entering us on his day-sheet as 'Casuals'. Such a description made us feel like vagrants, who had just booked in at a night-shelter, but Josie clearly meant no such thing; it was just his way of marking in visiting anglers, who were not hotel residents. I suppose we were vagrants in a sort of way, for we were staying in lodgings close by.

In the days that followed, we began to bring in some very respectable bags, and fairly soon found ourselves promoted from 'Casuals' to 'Mr Street and Mr Scorer'. Josie was keen that we should fill in the register each evening, as this was carefully scrutinized by prospecting anglers, and he wanted to be able to show better returns. In contrast to our previous year's results in The Rosses, we caught seventy-one white-trout between us (not including the harvesters returned) in thirteen days of fishing for a total weight of 88 lbs—a very reasonable average for Connemara waters—with twelve of our fish between 2 and 4 lbs.

There were two main rules on the Zetland waters, both of which met with our full approval—fly-fishing only was permitted and the use of outboard engines forbidden. Bill and I soon fell into an accustomed routine: we would call on Josie in the morning to find out the fishing he had allocated to us for the day. In the evening, after a change of clothes and supper at our lodgings, we would return to the Zetland, weigh our fish and leave them on the slab in the fishery office, to be collected later and put into the hotel's freezers. Then, with the day's sport duly entered in the register, we would spend the rest of the evening in the bar. Fishermen, of course, in a fishing hotel tend to talk fishing, which must often bore the ears off others there who do not fish. Most of us, however, are able to talk of other things, and many of these Zetland evening sessions stretched well beyond the bewitching midnight hour, sometimes, I confess, to the detriment of the next day's sport.

This routine was occasionally interrupted by other vagaries, as was the case when a twelve year-old German boy, who was staying at the hotel with his parents, became so impressed by the sight of a line of white-trout on the slab one evening that he more or less inveigled me into teaching him to fly-fish the following day. Young Heinz could speak some English, which was more than his parents could, but fishing in any of its forms was a closed book to all of them. The challenge of this young Teuton appealed to me, and I agreed to take him out next day—Josie was willing to fix him up with a rod and line. When I turned up the following morning at the pre-arranged time Josie was already under some pressure, as Heinz had been repeatedly asking,

'Vere is mein teacher? Vere is mein teacher?'

With the wind decidedly strong and freshening, I chose to take him onto one of the smaller loughs, and by the time we arrived at the boat it was blowing close to gale force: I told him we would have to fish from the shore. Such a wind was hardly what one would have asked for when showing a youngster, who had never held a fly-rod in his hands before, how to cast a fly. Heinz, however, soon got the hang of things, and was just about managing to get a short line out on the water with a single fly. In fact, he rose two small trout, but was much too slow to hook either of them. Knowing that results were expected, I decided after we had had our sandwiches, to take the oars and row him quietly round the edges of the lough, so that he could troll a team of flies behind the boat.

Dad, meanwhile, had been into Clifden for the day and stopped the car by the lough on his way home. I pulled the boat in and Heinz revealed his catch. Dad was clearly both impressed and delighted, but found it impossible to converse with me as I spoke no German. Instead, he addressed me in a far more universal language, thrusting a glass of vodka into my hands, and, when Heinz had finished his coke, the two of us resumed our task. That evening he proudly displayed his line of bog trout in the fishery office, making it quite clear to all-comers,

'I caught zem all; mein teacher, he caught none'.

We had both thoroughly enjoyed our day, though Josie was to put a slight damper on things, when Heinz asked about his fish;

'They'll do fine for the cat', was all he said.

I would like to believe that Heinz is a fly-fisherman today, but, living in Mannheim, I doubt that is so.

Most rods that were fishing the Zetland waters appeared to be concentrating on Gowla Lough, which held four boats, or else the various beats on the Owengowla River. The rest of the loughs seemed to have been seldom fished that season, and a few completely ignored altogether. By now, Bill and I had progressed from our status of casuals and become firm friends of Josie, who now cast us in a new role of pioneers, by suggesting that we should fish on those loughs that no-one had as yet visited at all, especially Big Athry, the larger of the two Athrys, and distant Anillaun, near the top of the Gowla system.

We knew next to nothing about Big Athry, which lay just off the road to Clifden, except that someone had described it to us as a 'difficult lough'. This information had only served to heighten our interest and whet our appetites. We were going to have to read it as best we could, and discover for ourselves the likely drifts. It only held one Zetland boat, and the amount of bailing this required provided yet more evidence that it was the lough no-one wanted to fish.

We were not on it for more than fifteen minutes before I was playing a lusty white-trout, which took a Peter Ross close in to the shore. With the fish safely netted, we both began to wonder what sort of omen this was to be on 'the difficult lough'. On any outing a white-trout on the first drift of the day raises the hope level but, being the fickle creatures that they are, it guarantees nothing. I have known days when it has turned out to be the only fish. The conditions were certainly promising, billowy clouds riding high above us, a warm breeze from the sea, giving a lively water, and the grape-dark summits of the Twelve Pins of Connemara rising clear behind us to the north.

There was much water to explore, and we soon began to make some interesting discoveries. As we rowed across the mid-part of the lough, over what we would normally have taken to be deep water, we began to spot areas of weed beneath us, some quite extensive. There were several such patches, and it was soon clear that this was where we should be fishing. Nowhere did this weed break the surface, so the area became difficult to pinpoint for subsequent drifts. The best we could do was to take approximate bearings on landmarks—a line of four cottages on the northern shore were helpful here—and to judge the distances. What we did find, however, was that, whenever we got it right, we moved fish over this middle ground.

At lunch time we pulled into the western shore with six fish already in the boat. Here we stretched out on the ferns and grasses that now covered an embankment of rocks—all that was left of the former Connemara Railway. Lazy cattle now grazed, where iron horses once had belched their smoke, as they towed their cargoes across the bogland. What a line that must have been, and what men that built it in the 1890's! Irish ballad songs still celebrate this marvellous railway.

(The guard talking to the driver:)

'Are ye right there Michael, are ye right?'
'Do ye think that we'll be there before the night?'
'Ye couldn't say for sartain, ye were so late in startin',
'But we might now Michael, so we might'.

'Are ye right there Michael, are ye right?'
'Do you think that ye can get the fire to light?'
'Oh an hour you'll require, for the turf it might be drier,'
'And it might now Michael, so it might'.

Later, we were to add another six to the bag with the Bibio,
fished on the bob, proving highly successful. The sixteen pounds
of white-trout, when laid out in the fishery office, made a fine
show and caused considerable interest to the resident anglers.
'Big Athry', of course, was our answer to the inevitable questions
people began to ask us. Not surprisingly, our outing was to start a
run on this lough and, since it only held one Zetland boat, Bill and
I found it hard to get back onto it. The run, however, was short-
lived, for the lough continued to prove its difficult self.

The following season, when we were out on it again, we came
across a man who lived in a big house by the shore and had his
own private boat there. If anyone knew the secrets of this place, it
must have been this fellow, and we had not moved a single fish by
the time we came up with him. He too had drawn a blank and,
sensing that we were complete strangers to the water, he said
ruefully, 'Do you know what the locals call this lough? They call
it 'The Penance'. Then, as a rider, he added 'Mind you, they do
say two men were on it last year and they took a dozen fish off it. I
cannot say whether they did or not, for I never saw them myself.'

Strangers though we were, Bill and I made no reply and wished
our friend well. Then, taking fresh heart from this uncorroborated
rumour, we returned to our own particular penance and the
search for those submerged beds of weed.

A fishery brochure in the hotel describes Gowla and Athry as
'loughs with the powers to bring men back from the ends of the
earth'. As I read it, I recalled that old mission hymn, and had
visions of the multitudes streaming back 'from Greenland's icy
mountains, from India's coral strand, where Afric's sunny
fountains roll down their golden sand'. In a brochure one may,
perhaps, excuse a measure of hyperbole, but Bill and I know it to
be true, at least where little Athry is concerned.

This lough is connected to its bigger brother, The Penance, by a short stream, and it too is skirted on its northern shore by the main Galway to Clifden road. At its north-eastern corner a smaller road, that leads off to Carna, joins this main highway, giving Little Athry its more usual name of 'Athry Crossroads'. Although in Connemara, one of the wildest tracts in Ireland, one could hardly fish in a more public place, at any rate in the month of August. I would guess that half of all tourists in the country will pass along that way at the height of the season. Whereas Big Athry is only partly visible from the road, Athry Crossroads is right alongside it and fully exposed.

It is impossible to catch a large fish there without drawing a crowd, and the bigger the fish the bigger the crowd. We had some previous experience of this only a few seasons before, when Bill had caught a large white-trout on little Salagh in The Rosses. Surprisingly for August, it turned out to be a kelt, thoroughly spent and in due course returned. The incident had coincided with the arrival on the road above of a large, green coach. Braking ominously, it had pulled up fifty yards above our boat, whereupon the doors opened to discharge the entire cargo, which consisted of elderly American dames. My immediate thought was that the sea had, at last, given up it's dead, that is until the dead grew ever more animated. Bright handkerchiefs now waved at us, cine-cameras whirred, all to the accompaniment of whoops and yells and toots on the motor-horn. These old dears probably imagined that Bill and I were employed by Bord Failte (Irish Tourist Board) to play a big fish here each week at the time of the green coach. They were, after all, on a scheduled 'mystery tour' in Erin's green isle.

My first large white-trout on the Crossroads was to show what it was really like to play before a truly international gallery. Anyone travelling that road is bound to notice a boat out, and also a sporting fish as it jumps clear into the air; it is when the two events are linked together that the traffic begins to stop. The fish I had hooked was all of three and a half pounds, fresh up from the sea and with all the energy of the oceans about him. Each time he leapt, he threw his silvered body in a shining parabola that arched over the water's top. Bill, at the oars, soon had the boat out in the centre of the lough, not to please the growing ranks, which were starting to line the shore, but to stop the fish from bolting for the weedbeds.

The main artery to the west had now ceased to throb, and began to take on the appearance of a display of ancient and modern transport; there were coaches, cars, tractors, gaily painted, horse-drawn caravans, beloved of travelling folk, bicycles and tandems. Had that old Connemara railway still been running, I am certain that the Clifden express, in the best traditions of that grand old line, would also have come to a grinding halt. Only aircraft were missing, which was a pity considering Alcock and Brown, those pioneers of transatlantic flight, had grounded only a few miles from where we were.

For ten minutes or more the issue hung in the balance, with NATO allies and Common Market alike responding in a mounting excitement. Then, at last, Bill shipped the oars, rose to his feet and stood ready with the net. Aware that the moment of truth was now approaching, the shore fell silent, only to erupt into a crescendo of approval as a bar of bright, burnished steel was hoisted inboard. As usual, we dispatched our quarry quickly, removed the fly-hook and slid him under the boards of the boat. Then, thinking to take our leave with a wave of the hands, we pulled quietly for the farther bank.

With the matinee now over most resumed their journey, but others, still eager for a curtain-call, decided to follow us to the other side. Desiring only to be left in peace, yet unwilling to seem churlish, we pulled ashore to face our inquisitors.

'Was it a salmon?' 'Can we take a picture?' 'May we buy it?' 'How much?', and all in a confusion of tongues that would have put the Tower of Babel to shame; some indeed had travelled from the ends of the earth. Dredging our memories now for half-forgotten words of school French and German, and with much gesturing, we did out best to please, short of putting the fish on the open market. It would probably have ended up being boiled over a camp fire, and it deserved a better fate than that. More than likely the Zetland would send it down to Clifden where, over an oak fire, it would in due course be turned into smoked sea-trout.

It was only when the madding crowds had left that Bill and I could resume what Izaak Walton once had called 'the contemplative man's recreation', but honest Izaak had never fished the Crossroads in August. We realized then that we should have taken the hat round, a collection for 'The Disturbed Fishermen's Aid Society' might well have been worth having.

Later, I began to realise why the catching of a fish on a fly-rod should have aroused so much interest and excitement. For one thing, I suppose that most of those present had never seen a game-fish in its natural habitat, let alone a fly-fisherman, and, even for those who had, there is still something profound and very elemental about the chase, that strikes a powerful, primitive chord in all of us. The more we have become moulded by living in a mass, industrialised, urban society the more deeply these natural instincts have become submerged, though never obliterated. We all still need the healing touch of nature and seek it in a whole diversity of ways, from looking after our pets, or watering the pot-plants, to strolling in the park. Paradoxically, we probably approach most closely when following the varied and traditional sports of the countryside.

Josie sent us to Anillaun, in order to discover whether or not the white-trout had yet reached that far up the system, and also to check on the boat there, which had suffered damage in the past from so-called joy-riders—'vandals' Josie had called them. It is a remote and isolated water, involving an hour's trek over a flat and yielding bogland, spongy enough to cause suction at every step and tiresome walking. We searched it thoroughly for about three hours and, though we found the small trout more than usually active, we only caught two white-trout, both small harvesters and duly returned. The conditions were good, and I am sure that, had the bigger fish been up there, we would have come across one or two of them.

We managed, however, to salvage the day by picking up six better fish on Redman's Lough, which lay below, and where, at one stage, we found ourselves playing three fish all at the same time. Anillaun had a decent enough stream running out of it, and would certainly have been well worth fishing after the next good rise in levels. Unlike Big Athry our visit had singularly failed to spark off another run on the boat.

The day, however, was memorable for quite another reason. To get onto the bog in the first place, we had gone down the gentle slope of a hill and were soon treading a cobbled way, now well overgrown with moss and grasses. As I stood there and looked around me, I began to feel ill at ease, as though some spirit or spirits, from the past had touched me. On every side were broken walls and nettle-grown foundations; browsing cattle, all unaware of the times that had been in it, scratched their sides against the crumbling masonry, twitching their tails; rough-laid stones divided tiny pastures, pocket handkerchief fields, that had been formed and fashioned over and around the unrelenting granite base. The view beyond the bog was superlative, as distant waters shimmered in the light of the sun, like jewels against the outline of mountain fingers clutching at the skies. I knew that others before me had stood where I was standing, and seen the same familiar sights, which had scarce changed down the centuries. Somewhere an ass brayed, its discordant note drowning the dying wail of unseen curlew that trembled on the summer air: both voices held the echoes of a dark, forlorn tragedy.

Then I began to see again a cluster of little homesteads, as once they were, with roofs of turf and hard-packed floors of mud, wisps of blue smoke curled to dance and vanish in the sky, chickens scattered noisily, as laughing children ran at play. So it had been, until the years the potato crops began to fail. Then one by one these hearths turned cold, the windows darkened and the voices stilled. Here were Bill and I setting out on a summer's day to fish a lough for pleasure, for food we had no need of, and now we trod the grave of what once had been a happy settlement.

Like many another, it was ravaged and destroyed by the Great Famine of 1845-48, a dreadful visitation that dealt death by starvation and fever to a million Irish people, and forced many more to emigrate to America, some so weakened by hunger that they never completed the passage. A population of over eight million in 1845 was reduced to six-and-a-half million by 1848; within a span of three years one fifth of the population had either died or emigrated. In the wake of this catastrophe what had been a trickle of emigrants now became a tidal flood, which only the recession of modern times, with its consequent lack of employment everywhere, has begun to stem.

Even before the famine years, the lives of the people in the less fertile regions of the west and south had been wretchedly poor and harsh. Here, by the mid-nineteenth century, half the population were living, or existing, on the bare subsistence supplied by the potato crop. It was struggle enough to feed their families and animals, and, even to keep their humble homes, they still had to pay the landlord's rent.

Imagination may have conjured up the scene for me, but it could never convey the grinding poverty, the hunger and fear of eviction, let alone the grief and despair that followed the wasting years. The unease that settled on me was caused not just by the misery of these undeserving people, but, even more so, by the sheer ineptitude of the British Government of the day. There was no need for it ever to have been as it was.

Gowla is the largest and most beautiful of all the Zetland waters with its ample spread of islands, bright with the flowers of heather, furze and honeysuckle and the fruits of bramble and mountain ash, little passages and long, hidden bays with secret entrances to lead you into them. It enjoys a further advantage in that virtually all its great expanse is fishable water, and its many drifts afford an ever-changing scene. It is also the most popular lough on the fishery, where four boats can fish all day with ease and scarcely one will be in sight.

If you want to know the flies to use on Gowla, then Bill Scorer is the man to consult, for, whenever the stalwarts are letting us down badly, he always seems to produce the fly that will do the trick. His changes are invariably bold in the extreme, but time and again they bring him fish and usually very handsome ones. Whilst I continue to flog away with textbook patterns, bravely ignoring the cramp that has got into my loins, Bill is surreptitiously scanning the fly-wallets and that magic black box he has. It has got to the stage now that I hardly dare ask, after one of his sleights of hand during a forlorn period, what he has got on the end of his line, in case I should injure myself further with disbelief or laughter. Even if he told you, you would scarcely believe it from the rational man he is, and yet I know I fish with new heart whenever he makes a change.

Gowla, along with all the best loughs of Ireland, or anywhere else for that matter, can become desperately dour at times, and I suppose the only tactic then is to try and wake the fish up with something really startling—shock-treatment for comatose fish.

Take, for example, the day in late August, which already had the feel of autumn about it, when we were drifting on a hidden bay, still known as 'Beat Eight', with the waters as lifeless as we had ever known them. Bill was soon consulting his oracles, whilst I persevered, for I knew no better. When I next surveyed the scene, there he was dapping a brilliant Yellow Mayfly, which rode the black waters like a first, bright primrose of spring. If any mayfly had fallen onto Beat Eight in the last twelve months, this must have been the one: it is true that I have seen a lone mayfly flutter over our boat in August, though it may have been only the ghost of a mayfly, for it looked too ethereal to be real. The late F. M. Halford, and all the other great purists of the English chalk-streams, must have been turning in their graves. Yet, before Bill's Mayfly had had time to get properly wet, it all happened. The two and a half pound white-trout was the only fish from Gowla that day.

Bill's changes, however, are invariably based on a sound angling philosophy, as well as a good understanding of a fish's essential psyche. He has proved, beyond doubt, that, on certain days, and in certain conditions of light, the Yellow Mayfly can be an excellent dap for a white-trout on an acid lough, for I have seen him catch several with it. Its success illustrates the basic divide that exists between white-trout and brown trout angling.

A white-trout does not know that a Mayfly is a mayfly—to him it is something totally unfamiliar and quite beyond his ken. He takes it, not because he is fond of mayflies, but because its colour, form and movement awake some dormant faculty and trigger a reaction, so that it acts as a simple lure. I very much doubt, however, whether a Mayfly dapped in August would evoke the same response from a big brown trout on the great limestone waters. One might be tempted up to have a look at it, but on finding it to be a Mayfly, suspicion would set the alarm bells ringing: to prove the point, of course, one would need to be dapping it in August on Mask or Corrib or Arrow, and I cannot see many willing to do that, when there are daddies and hoppers around.

As far as white-trout are concerned, I think that Bill has proved his case, and that too many of us have become needlessly hidebound and unimaginative in our approach.

There is one other seldom used 'fly' that works on Gowla, as I was to discover, when once more we found ourselves in the doldrums, this time near the head of the lough, where the little river enters from Redmans. At the start of a drift Bill announced, with all the assurance of a latter-day Archimedes, that this was the light to try the 'Scorer Green'. Readers may not know this fly, so a word of introduction is needed. Bill's father had originally conceived it in Appleby many years earlier, and I do not think he would have been offended, were I to describe it as being somewhat rough-tied. The dominant colour had been, and to some extent still was, green—the green of fresh-grown grasses. On the strong wind the boat was moving fast and soon there was only enough time for one more cast, before it was my turn to take to the oars, but time enough for Bill to land his green concoction right next to a vertical rock, which marked the absolute end of our drift. Here it was seized in no uncertain manner by a fine fish, whose voracity was to prove the undoing of the only Scorer Green that had ever existed. Following this, Bill had no alternative but to pension it off, and the breed became extinct after that.

Back in the fishery office that evening, I felt I was being more than a little disrespectful, as I wrote the words 'Yellow Mayfly' in the final column of the daysheet, under the heading 'Notes', though I did have my tongue in my cheek when I added 'Best fish 2lbs 14oz on a Scorer Green'. Josie supplemented the fishery's income by selling nylon and a selection of white-trout flies, and these sales were often boosted by the 'Notes' column on these sheets. It was not long before he was being asked for the Scorer Green, but could only reply that he was right out of stock!

A white-trout of the calibre of this one was certainly no fool of a fish, and yet he had stirred from his lie beneath the heather-covered rock on a day when none of his associates was moving. What was it that awoke his consciousness and disturbed his slumbers to make him grab the little 'green feller'? Sigmund Freud was no icthyologist, though he understood better than most men the source-springs of behaviour: had he been in our boat he might might well have suggested that from the deep, dark regions of that white-trout's animality there appeared a grass-hopper. Perhaps I have been too hard on the poor old Scorer Green for, if the Freudian premise is correct, then that would truly endow it with a lasting merit.

It was as we rowed through the channel between two of Gowla's islands that I spotted a group of small birds, four in all, which were making short bursts of flight between groups of trees on either island, breaking out into a shrill and playful chatter each time they landed. They were, in fact, a family of young merlins that had been reared in the old nest of a hooded crow, which their parents had commandeered. They are the smallest, and in many respects the most charming of all our falcons—the handsome tiercel being scarce bigger than a blackbird: it was once the lady's bird of falconry. This particular clutch, which I was to observe over several days, was probably still being fed by parents, but would in a short time be leaving home for good, as the family broke up, with each departing to seek a territory of its own.

In contrast to his cousin, the kestrel, which has proliferated in recent years through its ability to adapt to the urban environment, now colonizing the motorways and nesting in towers in the very heart of cities, the merlin is less able to adapt. He is essentially a creature of the true wilderness, those regions which man's encroachment is gradually whittling away, and, for this reason, remains under sore pressure: there is no way he can emulate his larger cousin and become a 'city gent'. I can think of few spells, more inward to my being, than to catch a brief glimpse of him in darting, twisting flight as he chases his prey—usually a meadow pipit—low above the heathers. This rare, demure falcon—true little prince of the moorlands—seems to embody the very spirit of all wild places, and I love him dearly.

Chapter 12

The Quare Place

I n most mountainous areas the locals tell tales of remote, high lakes beneath the clouds where large trout may be caught, but how to find them is quite another matter. Perhaps the most you can expect is a vague sweep of the hand towards some distant ridge of hills—'Up there', they say. Such places, by the very nature of their wildness, have no roads nor tracks to lead you to them. It is likely that your informant has never even seen the place, but is merely passing on a legend told him by his father. Or, if he is a fisherman himself, he may well want to keep the secret, so that his sons too will be able to fish it in their time, and who can blame them for this reticence? For one thing only is certain— were their names and routes to become public knowledge, they would in a very short space of time cease to be the 'quare' places that they are.

In general, high altitude lakes with their peaty waters teem only with small trout: mature and capable of spawning they may be, but the scarcity of food confines their growth and they remain a stunted breed. Other lakes, whose beds contain decomposing matter, are still producing gases and hold only few fish; those they have will be dark and of poor condition. Neither are worth the long, steep haul just to fish them. Some may even contain no fish at all, being poisoned by a combination of natural factors.

If these then are the normal run of high, mountain lakes, how is it that the odd one here and there can produce fine, deep-bodied trout of one to five pounds in weight with firm pink flesh? Such waters, though still of relatively low pH content, will have a different ecology altogether. They will certainly contain more plant life of their own, which in turn sustains a diversity of insects, and allows the sedge and caddis to flourish: these, together with beetles and crustaceans, form the main part of the diet of mountain trout. In the depths of winter they face near starvation and must survive on the reserves built up during the previous summer, but, as the season progresses and the waters begin to warm to the sun, so the food supply begins to increase once more. It is this diet that produces the fine pink flesh.

Even in lakes such as these, the balance of nature is so finely poised that it can easily be tipped. Overfishing can do it, as can unscrupulous men who care nothing for the ways of nature. These fellows, who scarce deserve the name of fishermen, will have their todays and let all the tomorrows go hang. Once the delicate balance has been seriously disturbed, the fishing will have gone for good. Only a long and painstaking process of restoration can bring it back again, and who will undertake such work in these far-off places? What would be the point anyway, once the gangs of raiders had beaten their path to it? Small wonder then that the few real fishermen, who know and love these places well, will guard their secrets jealously.

It was a chance remark from Dessie Sweeney in the bar one night that first aroused our interest in the 'quare' place. Many years had passed since he himself had climbed up to it. He too had been lured by stories of the big trout that had their home there, but he remembered the day so well for quite another reason: it was the only time he saw the golden eagle in all the majesty of its native habitat. Today, alas, this fine bird has long departed from the skies and crags of Donegal, but somewhere in the fastness of those hills the quare place still remained. Did the big trout still swim there? Did anyone go up to fish it? Bill and I decided to find out.

From all accounts it was a long and arduous ascent. Our first reconnaissance proved successful, but not before we had spent the best part of a day tramping the hills. Had we had a one-inch map to guide us we would have got there much sooner. The quarter-inch we had was of little help, as it was too small a scale to read the contours nicely. Instead, we had to rely on our own intuition and, perhaps, a sighting of the lake below us as we traversed the mountain ridge.

The day was fine and warm and, with the initial climbing over, we were glad to ease the burdens from our shoulders and lie down for a breather. The view was magnificent, endless acres of barren moorland, coloured by heathers and bog cotton, the white volcanic cone of Mount Errigal, the highest peak in Donegal, and

188

out, beyond the Bloody Foreland, to the wide Atlantic. No sign of human life or habitation: and certainly no sign of the quare place either. Did it really exist at all, or was it just a figment of the imagination, even a practical joke? Dessie was quite capable of pulling one on us.

For a few moments we must have lapsed into reverie. We were, however, soon recalled from our dreaming by the faint, but quite clear, sounds of music being played. The piping seemed to be coming from out of the heather. Bill and I in our own ways are fairly level-headed types, not the sort to be easily won over by stories of 'the little people', but our ears were not deceiving us now. We sat listening to the sweet notes of the pipe—only there was no piper. After all, I suppose that, if the 'wee folks', so beloved of Celtic lore, really did exist, this was just the sort of spot you would expect to come across them, and the day was grand too. Neither of us spoke for fear the music would go away.

It turned out to be a lone shepherd lad some sixty yards below us. We might never have spotted him at all, in which case we would have to have found some other explanation for the music. It is not difficult to see how some stories come to be told and handed down. Even so, my mind is not entirely closed to the possibilities of 'the little people'; some years later I was to have a stranger experience, and again it was on the climb to the quare place.

We passed the time of day with our young friend, and were happy to learn that the object of our search did in fact exist, but we had a good way yet to go. Already, our lengthening shadows told us there would be little time left for fishing. With a new-found spring in our step, we now followed the contours, gradually losing height as we went. Each new skyline raised our hopes only to dash them as the next appeared. Would the lake never show itself? In fact it never did until we were right beside it. We began to feel as those ancient pilgrims must often have felt, who longed for nothing more than just a glimpse of Mecca. Then suddenly there it was, stretched out before us at our feet. The day's exertions were now rewarded in full measure.

Cupped in a deep hollow of the mountains, it looked as if giant hands, in some primaeval dawn, had chiselled it from out the native rock. The scattered chippings still lay at random where they fell to form a shore line. On one side, guarding it like a fortress, the rock rose upwards for eight hundred feet to a forbidding precipice: on these heights the golden eagles may have built their eyrie. Today it is the home of ravens, and the noble peregrine is no stranger here. The heavy rains that drove against it, poured their waters directly into the lake below; a steep gully also drained this mountain, finally losing its waters to the lake in one last despairing leap. Apart from this, another brief and shallow stream also ran in; some trout may have spawned in this one, though we were to find little evidence of spawning over the years.

The lake was not a mile in circumference, but gave plenty of scope for two rods to fish. In such a natural amphitheatre sounds carried easily, so that Bill and I, fishing on opposite shores, could communicate across the water. What little shallows there were soon fell away and the lake was clearly of great depth: only in the corner by the waterfall were there short stretches of sand with patches of weed growing just beyond them. This was the corner where Bill was to have his greatest triumphs.

Weary from the climb, we sat down on a rock to take in the scene before us and to finish what was left of our food. I think that ancient sculptor must have had anglers in mind when he left this massive boulder on the shore; the size of a juggernaut and with a flat top, it lay midway on the northern side some thirty feet above the water. From this vantage-point it was possible to survey the whole lake, and, each time that we have climbed to fish here, this platform rock has made our base camp.

Now, as we scanned the surface, we saw the evidence we had come to seek. Here and there across the water small concentric circles, now widening now fading, told us beyond doubt that the big trout were still in it. How big they went we had yet to discover, but they certainly were not the stunted fellows that plagued us on the sea-trout loughs. Our joy, however, was to be short-lived. With the sun already on the western skyline, we remembered that our car was on the farther side of the mountains. The shortest route to it lay directly up that steep gully behind the waterfall, if only we had the energies to clamber up it. After the best part of a day's hike we had found the quare place: we had come to it on two feet: now to climb the gully we left it on all fours.

In the course of time we got the climb worked out to a nicety. The best approach by far started from the other side of the valley and, going at a steady pace, took two hours. It falls naturally into three phases, the first and last being steep and tiresome with the middle one offering a brief respite. From the spot where the car has to be left, the immediate skyline contains a contorted mountain ash, whose wind-blown arms beckon us to its rocky base. Looking back from this point we take a final glimpse of our car, now reduced to the proportions of a Dinky toy.

Once over this ridge, the route begins to level out and I christened this stage 'The Pampas'; here we cross swampy grassland where patches of bright, emerald-green moss conceal water-holes just waiting to swallow up the unwary. This leads us to a small and shallow lake, the lake of the red trout, which is full of tiny trout, and its chief interest is a stone shelter with a corrugated-iron roof built out over it. This still contains a table and bench and the remains of some old cutlery. I have no idea what its purpose was, but it was some achievement to have built it at all. Perhaps it had served as a lunch place for parties of shooters, or maybe was just a shelter for the shepherds.

Leaving the lake of the red trout, the climb enters its third and final phase, a steep slog over the shoulder of the mountain. It is a stage that is full of hazards, for knee-high heather hides many gaping holes, and you only know they are there when you fall into them. The hillside here is strewn with large rock boulders, which probably caused the holes in the first place, as they fell and tumbled down the mountain. I once took Kevin Bonner from Dungloe to fish the quare place with me; being a strong fifteen year old and used to working all day in the fields, he thought nothing of the climb. Even so, I had a friendly bet that, before we had reached the lake, he would have measured his length three times, nor was I wrong. The angler who goes alone to fish there really ought to leave word behind him where he is going. All alone and with a broken leg, it would be impossible getting back to civilisation and small chance of being found.

The mountain and the bog are full of meadow pipits, which are forever bobbing up ahead of us as we make the climb, but it is for the red grouse that we always keep our eyes open. Some years ago we would have put up two or three small groups, which whirred up from beneath our feet with a great clatter, voicing their alarm as they went, but they were never plentiful. Five years ago, I stirred one solitary cock and since then we have not seen any. These moors are not keepered, the old heather is no longer burnt off and I suppose the few hardy birds that barely held their own have been seen off by the hooded crows and the fox. We often came across a hare or two, and sometimes several head of deer, which had escaped the fencing round Glenveagh Estate. We know we will find the ravens overhead, but I am always delighted to see the tiny, little wren as well; fifteen hundred feet up, he is hardly in his usual habitat, yet he seems very much at home, as he flits in and out of the heather stalks beside the lake.

What one does not find are fellow human beings. On one visit I was almost at the lake when my eye caught sight of something in the heather just ahead. At first I took it for a piece of litter and went over to investigate; my fear was that the townees must have found our secret place at last. When I got there it was a one pound note, an English one at that, crisp and clean, and within a matter of a few seconds, I had gathered up another four of them. Since being very small, I had been brought up to believe that money did not grow on trees, but what was this? Had I been wrongly taught? Perhaps, after all, there was some magic plant that actually produced the stuff, and, if so, I need never work again. Surely it could not be.'the little people'? They would be altogether above (or perhaps below) this kind of thing. Anyway, it was our kind of money rather than their's, whatever their's might be. I may never know where it came from.

Many place-names in the remote, wilderness regions of our islands, even if we cannot pronounce them, spring from a history or mythology, long lost. In these lonely hills the 'voices' still speak to us and I have heard them. Never audible in the sense that wild birds are, they impinge, rather, as echoes or emanations that break in upon our consciousness. I have often wondered from what sources they came. It is, perhaps, no strange thing that folklore has peopled these uplands with elf-like creatures— fairies, little people, leprechauns—call them what you will. These 'wee folk' of legend seem to me never to have enjoyed an existence of their own, either natural or supernatural. They have always been flights of whimsy, created to give substance to a shared experience that seemed to evade explanation.

The day Bill and I usually choose for the quare place is a fine warm one, anticyclonic weather when the glass is high and steady, and the chance of rain, small. Such a day means we can leave the waterproofs behind. The less we have to carry the better. Even the contents of the fishing bags are carefully scrutinised before we leave the car. Essential tackle and enough food and drink are all that is needed, with the added luxury of a pair of field-glasses. My net is folded and put into the rucksack, but Bill makes his own nets, and the stout hazelwood handle doubles up well as a walking-staff. The right kind of day needs a little breeze in it as well. On a few occasions we have been caught up there when the wind has died completely. The midges then make life intolerable, and I know nothing that will deter the Irish bog midge so well as a breeze. You can light a fire, mask your face, neck and ears in a net, blow clouds of tobacco smoke from the old pipe and put on every kind of repellent on the market, but the blighters still attack. They have not read the ICI label on the bottle!

When the frigate and troopship HMS *Birkenhead* went down off South Africa on 26th February, 1852, in order to enable the women and children to be got safely away in the boats, the Royal

Marines' Band played and the Royal Marine Detachment formed up and drilled to the very end. Rudyard Kipling wrote in his poem, 'To stand and be still to the *Birkenhead* drill is a damn tough bullet to chew, but they done it, the Jollies, 'er Majesty's Jollies, soldier and sailor too.' And so it was, but I have yet to meet the man who can stand and be still on an Irish bog when these lads are really on the rampage. The boat fisherman is more fortunate, for midges do not come out over the water, but even he must run the gauntlet in the end. Perhaps a battery-operated fan, attached to a helmet, might work, though it would be an awkward brute to carry, and, should one fall in, might well act as a propeller, driving one feet-first into the middle of the lake. For any inventive entrepreneur the anti-midge market remains a wide open one.

The other reason for choosing a fine, warm day is that we both like to put up the dry-fly when we get there. On just such a day in August the trout will be rising. After the climb we slake our thirst on the platform rock, and soon will have spotted half a dozen good fish or more. Just out from the corner, where the shallow river enters, there is an outcrop of rock in the lake, and invariably a trout shows there, but he will be well out of range. These are cruising trout and that gives some hope. They are also territorial and appear to have their own clearly defined beats, which they patrol up and down in a leisurely way about eighteen inches below the surface, just like old-fashioned policemen on the beat, as they pick off whatever food offers on the surface. Soon, with rods at the ready, Bill and I part company and set off for different parts of the shore. Both of us will have spotted a fellow we want to try for.

Our experience here suggests that even these large trout are not all that selective as regards the flies: a big trout rising on the river will be much more choosy. Compared with his counterpart on the quare place he will, in fact, be thoroughly spoilt. The hatches of fly on most rivers are prolific, and the fish settle to feeding on that particular fly, which is hatching, ignoring all else. By contrast, the hatch, such as it is, on the high lake will be quite different. The flies here will be sparse and various, many of them land-bred insects, blown by the breeze onto the water, and the fish must search them out. The river trout has no need to search, but lies still and waits for the armada to sail over him. It is the difference between the man who feeds in a restaurant and the man who goes out shopping, comes home to cook and has to wash up afterwards.

The size of fly, however, does matter. Quite recently I was fishing for one of these big patrolling trout, casting out my fly on the observed line of his travels and leaving it out on the water. I was, in fact, casting to about the limit of my length. Because of this I had put up rather a large fly in order to be able to see it more easily. I hate to lose sight of the fly and, with the pin-ripple on the water and the changing shadows, as the sun goes in and out of cloud, that often happens. When the fish did come I could see that he was thoroughly suspicious of it: he gave it a close look, nosing all round it, even tried to drown it with a splash of his tail and finally left it altogether. Something was wrong. I changed at once to a smaller, hackled fly and cast out again. Nothing happened for a long time. Meanwhile Bill, unbeknownst to me, had moved back onto the platform rock from where he now called over to me. I glanced his way, and in that brief moment the fish took my fly. There was nothing I could do about it, for, by the time I came alive, the fish had well and truly rejected it.

The lesson, of course, is never to take your eyes off the dry-fly, for it is certain that Murphy's Law applies to fishing just as much as to any other human activity. This is the law that deals with the question of probabilities. Murphy was an American teacher, but he must have had more than a trace of the Irish in him. To test the law of probability he told his class of thirty students to butter thirty slices of bread with peanut butter. These were then thrown into the air to see if fifteen would land on their dry sides and fifteen on their buttered sides, or whatever the ratio might be. In fact twenty-nine landed buttered sides down and the other one never came down at all. It did not go into orbit, but merely stuck fast to the ceiling.

Fortified by such experiments, he confidently announced his law, which states that, if anything can possibly go wrong, it almost certainly will do so. Sometimes I feel that it is a law that works specially for fishermen, or rather against them. How often have I watched hardy North Sea anglers legering for cod with their six ounce weights in bitter winter weather with never a bite all morning, but the moment they start to light a pipe, or pour out a mug of steaming soup from the flask, the rod top goes berserk. Murphy can induce a fish to take just as surely as the most skilful nymph fisherman can.

With luck, it is possible to catch the quare place on a day when the daddy-longlegs (crane fly) are being blown onto the lake in good numbers. This offers a real bonanza for the trout. On any day in August the odd daddy will be on the water, but I have never found them there in any quantity. Bill did find it so on one occasion when he had gone there on his own, and the trout were fairly walloping them. He lost no time in putting up the artificial daddy and was soon casting. Within a short space he had risen at least eight and failed to connect with a single one. By this time the daddies were getting fewer and the trout were beginning to lose interest. Now Bill is a pretty useful operator on the whole, and it was only when he came to reel in that he discovered the hook shank had broken off his daddy. In the excitement to get started, he must have hit one of the many boulders on the shore with his backcast, which is all that is needed to do this.

Every fly-fisherman knows this experience and few can be more mortifying. There is certainly no need to check the fly every time a fish is missed, but I am equally beginning to learn that there are distinct times when a check is called for. These are the occasions when you know the fish has taken properly only to let go again after a fraction of a second. I lost two such trout in quick succession on the river recently, and kicked myself afterwards. I knew I should have checked the first time and, of course, the hook had broken.

The quare place was to show me two of the biggest trout I have ever seen outside a glass case. Young Kevin and I had just finished our climb, and were taking it easy on the platform rock, when the water suddenly erupted right below us at the very edge. This was followed by a great V wave, which continued for a quarter of the way across the lake. It seemed more akin to a submarine than a fish. My first thoughts were that it was an otter, but the appearance of a tail and dorsal fin soon revealed a trout of at least six pounds in weight. On a different visit I startled another of the same proportions, which, once again, was feeding right in at the shore-line. He could, of course, have been the same fellow. There is no doubt that the trout of the quare place do come in very close, especially where the water is still deep, and that they forage for beetles on the rocks at the very margins of the water. Several autopsies have shown this item to be a prominent feature in their diet.

Neither Bill nor I ever hooked a fish of this class up there, though Bill did catch two memorable ones, each time when fishing on his own. Both captures had more than an element of luck about them. On the first occasion he had done little up to late afternoon, when he spotted one of the big fellows making a slow cruise some distance out. Bill moved up to his favourite corner under the steep mountain, close by the place where the waterfall tumbles. More for something to do than for any other reason, he decided to change his fly and, searching the lapel of his jacket, he pulled out a small brown one, a thoroughly nondescript job, and tied it on. He cast well out, left his fly to sit on the water and then sat down himself on the rock ledge. Nothing disturbed the peace for a long time.

When the cruiser finally did return, instead of the usual hearty rise, he stuck up his nose and gently sucked the fly down, barely ruffling the surface at all. Bill raised his rod to tighten on him and then, as he described it to me later, felt as though he had offended against the universe. The reel went mad as the fish tore off into the centre of the lake, running some eighty yards and stripping all of the line and most of the backing. No amount of finger-braking on the drum of his reel could slow this charge, and Bill peered anxiously at his quickly emptying spool.

The fish, quite unaware that victory was only feet away, now ceased his run, and Bill began the long process of recovery. He then realised that he had left his net where he had last been fishing. Without it, and with such a small fly, he was beginning to rate his chances pretty low, but, if success looked slight, he was at least determined to get a good sight of the fish that he had hooked. Luck now played her card and the fish was safely beached. It was a fine deep trout, as all of them were, and weighed three pounds nine ounces.

The other big one was some three ounces lighter and was caught from the same spot, only on this occasion Bill had actually placed his rod down beside him on the rock. His thoughts may have wandered, but his eyes never left his fly as he smoked his pipe in the late afternoon sun. This fish too took just as quietly, allowing Bill time to grab his rod and tighten on him as he turned with the fly in his mouth.

In the case of the larger fish, Bill took some scales from below the dorsal fin and sent them, together with other measurements and details to the Inland Fisheries Trust (now the Central Fisheries Board) in the hope that their observations might throw more light on the big fish of the quare place. A curt reply informed him that the trout was four years old, a fact he had guessed anyway.

On the last day that we fished there together we were as usual on opposite sides of the lake. Bill had worked his way gradually into his favourite corner, which now removed him from my sight, though we were still in hailing range. All I knew was that he had spotted another cruising fish and was trying for him; the next signal told me he was into one. I had just taken a fish myself and was moving across the boulders to intercept another that had shown. It was then that I heard heavy sounds of splashing coming from the far corner. Immediately I thought that Bill had at last got stuck into one of the really big lads, only to discover later that the splashing was not caused by any monster trout but by Bill himself. The trout he had hooked had made a bee-line for a clump of weeds, from which he stubbornly refused to be moved. Bill had put his rod down, stripped off and swum out to see if he could remedy things at the far end. All that happened was that everything in the lake went down including the fellow I was stalking!

What was strange about the quare place was the apparent absence of any small fish there. If they were present we would surely have both seen and caught them. My two smallest each weighed $\frac{3}{4}$ lb. My own theory is that the great majority of young, spawned fish are systematically eaten by the larger ones, with only a few surviving to become the next generation of big trout. Trout of $\frac{3}{4}$ lb would almost have reached the size that would have given them safety from predatory parents. It seems that some kind of self-regulating equilibrium exists between numbers of trout and food available, and if this is so, it is but another example of nature's economy.

The average size of those we caught ranged between one and two pounds, and all beautifully marked. They fought like tigers too. I hooked two which bolted straight to the bottom, stripping the line as they went, and never moved again. The floor of the lake, like the shore line, seems to be composed of large boulders, and these trout clearly made directly for their rockfast sanctuaries. I tried all the tricks I knew, such as easing off the line-tension altogether, to persuade them to move but with no success. I was left with no alternative but to break. I have had the same experience with trout on Lough Mask, which has a similar bottom, but with a boat one can manoeuvre to alter the angle of pressure, and in time the fish will move out again.

On lakes such as the quare place, brother anglers are few and far between. Fortunately their main protection lies in their comparative inaccessibility. Hill-walkers, shepherds, deer-stalkers, a few geologists—these will know their whereabouts, but only a handful of anglers, whose sport is enhanced by the challenge of the climb, will both know and cherish their secrets as well. There is a man I know well in Dungloe, who would love to fish this lake beneath the crags, and I have invited him to come with me several times, but such is his disposition that he says he will only do it if a helicopter puts him down there.

I remember well the only other angler I ever met there. He was already fishing, casting out his team of wet-flies and working them quietly in the light breeze, when I arrived, hot and exhausted from the climb. After a pause I set up my single dry-fly and, putting a hundred yards between us, began to fish my way up behind him. I could see that the fellow ahead of me was getting on in years, partly lame and walking amongst the boulders with the aid of a stick. I admired him for being there at all. When we finally met up we fell to talking as anglers do, and I found out that he had known and fished this place for as long as he could remember. The years, however, were now beginning to take their toll—already he had left man's allotted span of three score and ten well behind him. He had made the climb, this day, resolved to see and fish it one last time. For him it was to be a final pilgrimage of thanksgiving and farewell.

Shortly before we met I had taken a good fish to the dry-fly, and how I wished it had come to his rod rather than mine. My heart began to fill with sadness as I watched him pack away his rod and start to prod his way with care down the little stream that left the lake. I thought to myself, 'There goes a true fisherman, a genuine sportsman, the very kind of fellow for whom God has fashioned all such quare places.'

But the old man may have been wiser than he knew. For Bill and I now know that other so-called fishermen have found our place. A recent visit has revealed the dreaded signs and confirmed our worst fears. No longer did we see the big trout rising as once they had, and the banks were strewn with litter. Anglers, who can spoil a place like this with their beer cans and bottles, cigarette packets and plastic bags, are just as ready to use any method known to them to remove the fish. Lobworms and spinners—to say nothing of otter-boards and other sinister devices—can ruin a lake, and especially one where the stock of good fish is holding its own by such a narrow margin: they ruin it for all true fishermen and equally, and more especially, for themselves as well. Yet nature remains amazingly patient and wonderfully resilient.

In February, 1968, I lay in the intensive care unit of a hospital, having suffered the traumas of a premature coronary. Forbidden even to turn over, I lay there with nothing to do but watch a TV screen at the end of my bed, which monitored my heart beat—a pretty dreary programme it was too. The only part of me which could still roam freely was my mind, and in those few days it kept turning to the quare place. I wondered if I would ever fish there again. Thank God, I have done so many times. One thing I know now—in the summers that remain, Bill and I will continue to climb the mountain with our rods, will stretch out on the platform rock and scan the water as we did so many years ago. Someday the trout will rise again.

Meanwhile in a corner of my former garden in Hartlepool there grew a white heather planted in the black bog soil of Donegal, brought back in a biscuit tin. It was the only cutting to take root from a sprig plucked from the shores of the quare place. Each summer it became a mass of flower, pure white, to fill my heart with joy and hope, as it raised my spirit and my thoughts to far off distant hills.

As a hopeful postscript to this chapter, I report that the big trout are once again rising on the quare place. Bill and I still linger there till the sun has kissed the rim of the western hills, when it will be time to start the homeward trek. We take no more than three trout with us—enough from such a water—but they are tokens of nature's indomitable spirit for recovery, and, perhaps also, signs, in days when the fishing scene everywhere is shadowed by the dark spectres of pollution and human folly, that all is not yet lost. The satisfaction they have given is incomparable for on the quare place we have, after all, been the guests of the gods.